First produced at the Hippodrol.., ~~..........., ~~p........ ....., 1951.

Production at the Palace Theatre, London on 20th October, 1951.

———

EMILE LITTLER'S

ZIP GOES

A MILLION

A MUSICAL EXTRAVAGANCE

IN TWO ACTS

(BASED ON AN IDEA BY WINCHELL SMITH AND BYRON ONGLEY)

Book and Lyrics by ERIC MASCHWITZ

Music by GEORGE POSFORD

Directed by CHARLES HICKMAN

FOR AMATEUR PRODUCTION ENQUIRIES

UNITED KINGDOM AND WORLD
EXCLUDING NORTH AMERICA
plays@samuelfrench.co.uk
020 7255 4302/01

Each title is subject to availability from Samuel French,
depending upon country of performance.

ZIP GOES A MILLION

Character		In Palace Theatre, London, Production
Sheriff MacOwen and Principal Dancer	Non-Singing - - - -	IAN STUART
Lilac Delany - -	Dancing. Contralto Low "A" to top "D"	BARBARA PERRY
Buddy Delany - -	Baritone. Low "A" to top "G"	WARDE DONOVAN
Jed Harper - -	Non-Singing - - -	JOHN MARQUAND
Motty Whittle - -	Non-Singing - - -	- WALLAS EATON
Sally Whittle - -	Mezzo. Low "A" to top "G"	- SARA GREGORY
Percy Piggott - -	Light Tenor. Low "B" to Top "F" Sharp	GEORGE FORMBY
George Connelly -	Non-Singing - -	- WILFRID CAITHNE
Paula Van Norden -	Non-Singing - -	PHOEBE KERSHAW
Hairdresser - -	Non-Singing - -	AUDREY FREEMAN
Manicurist - -	Non-Singing - -	DIANA RUSSELL
Barber - - -	Non-Singing - -	- JAMES BROWNE
Shoe-Shine Boy - -	Non-Singing - -	- KENNETH GRANVILLE
Eddie - - -	Non-Singing - - -	IAN STUART
James Van Norden -	Non-Singing - - -	- FRANK TILTON
The Musical Director	Non-Singing - - -	- JAY DENYER
1st Policeman - -	Non-Singing - -	- DONALD BAMFORTH
2nd Policeman - -	Non-Singing - -	XANDER HAAGEN
Lefty - - -	Non-Singing - -	JOHN MARQUAND
Touch - - -	Non-Singing - - -	- JAY DENYER
Elevator Boy - -	Dancing. Non-Singing -	JAMES BROWNE
Captain - - -	Non-Singing - -	- WILFRID CAITHNESS
Wireless Operator -	Non-Singing - -	JOHN MARQUAND
Kelly - - -	Non-Singing - - -	IAN STUART

Singing Girls. Singing Boys. Dancing Girls. Dancing Boys.

MUSICAL NUMBERS

Music by GEORGE POSFORD   *Lyrics by* ERIC MASCHWITZ

Orchestrations by DEBROY SOMERS

" Afternoon in Texas " - - - - - - - Ballet
" Saving up For Sally " - - - - - Percy and Chorus
(*Lyric by Eric Maschwitz and Emile Littler*)
" The Thing About You " - - - - Lilac and Buddy
" Ordinary People " - - - - - - Percy and Sally
(*Lyric by Eric Maschwitz and Emile Littler*)
" Zip Goes A Million " - - - - - Percy and Company
(*Lyric by Eric Maschwitz and Emile Littler*)
" It Takes No Time to Fall in Love " - - Sally and Buddy
" The Story of Chiquita " - - - - - Lilac, Girls and Boys
" Nothing Breaks But the Heart " - - - - - Buddy
" I Owe You " - - - - - - - - Percy and Sally
" Saving Up For Sally " (*reprise*) - - - - - - Percy
Office Ballet
" Trouble With My Heart " - - - - - Motty and Sally
" Zip Goes A Million " (*reprise*) - - - Percy and Company
" Raratonga " - - - - - - - Sally and Company
" Trouble With My Heart " (*reprise*) - - - Buddy and Boys
" Pleasure Cruise " - - - - - - Percy and Company
" Running Away to Land " - - - - Buddy and Boys
" Garter Girl " - - - - - - Lilac and Company
" Thou Art For Me " - - - - - Buddy and Lilac

COMPOSITION OF ORCHESTRA

AS AT PALACE THEATRE, LONDON

6 Violins	1 2nd Tenor Saxophone
1 Viola	doubling Clarinet
1 Cello	2 Trumpets
1 Bass	2 Trombones
1 1st Alto Saxophone	1 Percussion
doubling Clarinet	1 Guitar doubling Hawaiian
1 2nd Alto Saxophone	Guitar, Banjo and Mandolin
doubling Flute and Piccolo	1 Piano
1 1st Tenor Saxophone	
doubling Clarinet	

SYNOPSIS OF SCENES

ACT ONE

Playing Time.
Minutes

Scene 1 .... PIGGOTTSVILLE, TEXAS (33)
Scene 2 .... THE RITZ-CARLTON HOTEL, NEW YORK (7)
Scene 3 .... THE STAGE OF THE ZIEGFELD THEATRE (16)
Scene 4 .... AN ALLEY OUTSIDE (12)
Scene 5 ..... THE PIGGOTT OFFICES, ROCKEFELLER CENTER (30)

ACT TWO

Scene 6 .... RARATONGA (14)
Scene 7 .... THE SEA SHORE (4)
Scene 8 (a) .... ON BOARD " THE PLEASURE CRUISE " (10)
(b) .... " GARTER GIRL " (5)
(c) .... ON BOARD " THE PLEASURE CRUISE " (6)
Scene 9 .... NEW YORK (4)
Scene 10 .... THE PIGGOTT PENTHOUSE (9)

A SELECTION OF PRESS NOTICES FOLLOWING THE PALACE THEATRE, LONDON, PRODUCTION

" It took 30 seconds to make a West End audience whistle for more . . . it has the elegance of a Bond Street box with an Eccles cake inside . . . it is irresistible."—*Daily Express.*

" A real British Musical show."—*The Star.*

" This Emile Littler production at the Palace is a family show, with good humour, catchy songs, several smart girls, and a familiar story with a new twist. Moreover, it is well dressed and cleverly put together as the Littler shows are."—*News of the World.*

" ' Zip Goes A Million ' is a winner all the way. It has surpassed expectations beyond the wildest dreams of impresario or cast. ' Zip ' is just what any doctor would order for a wholesome, merry night out.—*Weekly Sporting Review.*

" This Musical Extravagance is Lancashire hot-pot served on a silver platter; a comic post-card (and a clean one) framed in gold."
—*Daily Mail.*

" This show does exactly what it sets out to do and will be a great success in consequence."—*Daily Telegraph.*

"A diverting show that looks set for a long run."—*Sunday Dispatch.*

" An enthusiastic audience gave the show a great reception."
—*Sunday Chronicle.*

CALL: MUSICAL DIRECTOR, DANCERS, SINGERS, LILAC DELANY, JED
HARPER, HANK, BUDDY DELANY, SHERIFF MACOWEN

WARN: Switchboard, Men in Flys, Bars in Front of House, Ring in
Orchestra

SWITCHBOARD CUE No. 1. House to half at end of National Anthem.

CUE No. 2. House out at end of Overture.

CURTAIN UP

ACT 1

SCENE 1 (Playing Time: 33 mins.)

PIGGOTTSVILLE, TEXAS   (Early Evening—end of August)

MUSIC CUE No. 1 AS PER SCORE

Characters in this scene:

LILAC DELANY, BUDDY DELANY, JED HARPER,
MR. CONNELLY, SHERIFF MacOWEN, M O T T Y
WHITTLE, PERCY PIGGOTT, HANK, SALLY WHITTLE,
SINGERS AND DANCERS.

A sleepy little square outside the Lone Star Hotel R.
and the Piggott House L. The Hotel is a primitive-
looking establishment with entrance up steps through
porch and side-entrance up stage with old-time swing-
doors into bar. The Piggott House is the ghost of a
fine old mansion with shuttered windows round and
over which bright bougainvillea has run wild. Upstage
of the house a narrow lane runs off to L. In the background can be seen the prairie with its oil derricks,
shimmering in the haze of late afternoon.

No. 1 BALLET "AFTERNOON IN TEXAS."

END OF OVERTURE. SWITCHBOARD CUE No. 3.

See Dance Plot.

WHEN THE CURTAIN RISES, *the scene is empty
except for one girl sitting on a form stage R eating an
apple and engrossed in a novel, and one man asleep
on hotel steps.*

Suddenly a COWBOY *leaps into the middle of the stage
with a wild " Yippee " from stage R below barricade.
Followed by all singers and dancers from all entrances.
They go into opening dance.*

AT END OF DANCE ENTER *from the L.U.E.* LILAC
and BUDDY.

CALL: MOTTY WHITTLE, SALLY WHITTLE,
PERCY PIGGOTT.

SHERIFF: He'll be here any moment now—and oh boy, what a
party !

(TEXANS *cheer, etc.*)

BUDDY:	(*To* SHERIFF) Pardon me, sir. (*Coming down stage L L.C. with* LILAC *on his Left*).
SHERIFF:	Howdy, stranger
LILAC:	*Is* this Piggottsville ?
SHERIFF:	It sure is!
TEXANS:	You bet, etc., etc.
BUDDY:	But our agent booked us to give a show at the Big Hotel here—
SHERIFF:	That 'ud be the " Lone Star," Mister. (*Points*). There she is !
BUDDY:	(*Gasping*) Get the Big Hotel!
LILAC:	I could *murder* that guy!
	(*Enter* JED *from Hotel*)
JED:	Howdy, folks ? Are you the vaudeville act I sent for ?
BUDDY:	Sure. The Dancing Delanys. Lilac.....
LILAC:	And Buddy !
BOTH:	Always on their Toes ! (*They both do a comedy time step*).
JED:	Jed Harper—owner of the Lone Star Hotel.
MAN 1:	(*Loud aside*) Always on the make! (TEXANS *laugh*).
JED:	How ! I got a nice double room for you.
LILAC:	Two singles please.
BUDDY:	We're only engaged! What kind of a show do you want us to put on here tonight ?
JED:	Well I reckon we might have a bit of a sing song (BOYS *and* GIRLS *shout* " *Yipee* ") and little missie here could dance with some of the boys. (BOYS *do a whistle*) (*Moving over to* LILAC'S *R*).
LILAC:	I beg your pardon ?
BUDDY:	I'll have you know Miss Delany is a lady! (*Pulling* JED *over to Stage R.C.*)
LILAC:	You're dam' right I am! (*Bus*) (*Folding her arms*).
BUDDY:	We're the Dancing Delanys and you act as if we were a couple of bums. Maybe you don't know it but we're a draw !
LILAC:	They wouldn't know what a draw was !
JED:	Is that so ? Lady, we have the biggest draw in Texas getting in on the train any minute now.
TEXANS:	(*Nodding excitedly*) Sure we have, etc., etc.
JED:	One guy arriving—with a million dollars.
LILAC: } BUDDY: }	(*Wide-eyed*) *A million* ?
JED:	Sure ! Old Man Piggott left a million dollars to his nephew Percy-val—from England !
LILAC:	I may be dumb but just who *was* " Old Man Piggott "?

SHERIFF:	The Big Oil Boss, lady.
JED:	You should have seen this town in *his* day ...
MAN 2:	Piggottsville was *something* then !
JED:	Drink—gambling—WOMEN !
SHERIFF:	Paris had nothing on Piggottsville ! (*Loud agreement from crowd*).
LILAC:	Too bad the Piggotts had to pull out !
SHERIFF:	Ah, but they're coming back !
TEXANS:	Sure—sure—etc.
JED:	This guy from England sure is going to wake things up !
SHERIFF:	That's what this town needs.
TEXANS:	Sure, etc., etc.
JED:	Yessir—money *flowing*. You don't know them Piggotts —they're jest natural born hell-raisers.
SHERIFF:	And can they *spend* ? We'll *all* be in the money !
BUDDY:	You seem mighty certain of that, Mister !
SHERIFF:	You bet ! Percy Piggott won't be no tight wad. He's a grand English Gentleman all the way from Lancashire.

(Motor horn sounds off stage)

JED:	He'll be easy picking Sheriff (*nudging* SHERIFF) if you get what I mean.
BUDDY:	Come on Lilac—get slicked up Honey—we're about to meet a millionaire !
LILAC:	I'd better get warmed up ! (*They both run off into Hotel. Up R.C.*)

(Motor horn sounds off stage L 2nd time)

MAN:	(*Entering hastily from L.U.E.*) Jed—Boys—the taxi's just comin' up the highway.

MUSIC CUE No. 1B, " ZIP GOES A MILLION " *for* PERCY'S *entrance.*

JED:	Gosh darn it—that'll be him. (*He runs to Flagstaff on L side of Hotel and hoists the Union Jack*).

> (*Great excitement and cheers from boys and girls who run up stage as* MOTTY *is carried on shoulder high from L.U.E.*)
>
> SALLY *follows. She carries bag and an umbrella.* MOTTY *is a little man, dressed very English with a bowler hat.*

MOTTY:	(*Struggling*) Hey, wait a minute. Stop it. Put me down ! You daft gormless lot. (*Etc., etc.*)
SALLY:	You got it all wrong ! (*Running round her Father and back to L.C.*)
TEXANS:	Welcome—Mr. Piggott !
MOTTY:	My name's Motty Whittle, I'm *not* Mr. Piggott.

SALLY:	No, he's not Mr. Piggott, he's my Dad ! (JED *lowers Union Jack*).
	(*Motor horn sounds off stage L.*)
ALL:	*Not* Mr. Piggott ?
MOTTY:	No. (*They drop him. Exclamations from* TEXANS). That's what I've been trying to tell you all the time. (SALLY *moves from C to L.C.*)
	Sounds of argument. Crowd faces upstage as ENTER PERCY PIGGOTT *from L.U.E., back to audience, in indignant argument with* HANK. *the cab driver.* PERCY *has bag, bundles, etc. (Music swells up when* PERCY *appears and fades when he speaks).* (JED *hoists Union Jack as* PERCY *appears*)
PERCY:	I won't have it—and I won't pay it. You can't diddle me, I come from Newton-Le-Willows. Four dollars, just from station—your clock must be fast. I've been in taxis before—twice. Four dollars! Motty! What's that in English money ?
	MOTTY *refers to a book—the kind that tourists abroad carry containing useful phrases with their foreign equivalent.*
MOTTY:	Twenty-eight shillings.
PERCY:	(*Appalled*) Twenty-eight shillings ! (*To Taximan*) I'll give you half-a-crown.
	(SALLY *gives taximan a five dollar note and he exits L.U.E.*)
JED:	Welcome to Piggottsville, Mister. My name's Jed Harper.
PERCY:	Pleased to meet you, Mr. Harper. (*Grumbling*) Four dollars.
JED:	And welcome to *you*, Mrs. Piggott. (*Moving over to* SALLY).
SALLY:	(*Embarrassed*) But I'm not Mrs. Piggott.
PERCY:	Not yet ! But you never can tell !
SALLY:	Percy, please. You mustn't.
PERCY:	This is Miss Sally Whittle.
SALLY:	How d'ye do.
JED:	Howdy, Miss Whittle. (*Shakes her hand*).
PERCY:	And her dad, Motty Whittle.
JED:	Howdy, Motty. (*He moves over to* MOTTY *R.C. holding out his hand and short-sightedly passes him—he turns back and shakes* MOTTY'S *hand*).
MOTTY:	How d'ye do.
PERCY:	We all come from the same place.

Opening Ballet—PIGGOTTSVILLE, TEXAS
Doors and windows practical.

Act 1 : Sc. 1.

'Lilac' and 'Buddy'
feature "The Thing
About You."
Act 1 : Sc. 1.

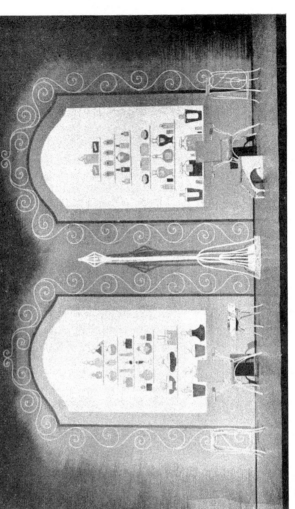

RITZ CARLTON HOTEL, NEW YORK.

Act 1 : Sc. 2.

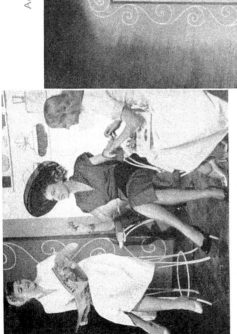

' Paula Van Norden ' hears about ' Percy Piggott ' from her hairdresser and manicurist.   Act 1 : Sc. 2.

SALLY:	Aye, we're from (*proudly*) Newton-Le-Willows.
MOTTY:	Aye, *the* Newton-Le-Willows.
PERCY:	Aye, there's not many places like Newton-Le-Willows.
MOTTY: } SALLY:	No !
JED:	(*To* MOTTY) You a relation, Mister ?
SALLY:	(*Laughing*) Percy worked for Dad.
MOTTY:	Aye, best window cleaner in Lancashire is our Percy. And when we heard about his little bit of luck, I says to Sally, " If Percy's going all way to Texas, *we're* going with him to keep an eye on him."
SALLY:	That's right.
PERCY:	And a good job you came. Four dollars !
MOTTY:	Aye, you have to be careful.
JED:	Mister, I keep the Lone Star Hotel—best liquor in town. When are you throwing the party ?
PERCY:	Party ? It isn't Christmas . . .
JED:	We've got three rooms all ready fer you. (*Picking up bags and moving up to Hotel*).
MOTTY:	*Three* rooms ? You can make it *two*, lad. Percy and me can muck in together !
PERCY:	Can't I have a bed to myself ?
MOTTY:	What for ?
PERCY:	Well, I'm a big lad now!
SALLY:	You have it, if you want it, Perce.
MOTTY:	(*To* SALLY) Come, come, Lass. He's not made of money, He's no 'but one million.
PERCY:	Aye, he's right, Sally. I may have a bit of brass now, but you never know what'll happen, and when I've had talk with lawyers, back it all goes into Penny Bank at Newton-Le-Willows. (PERCY *moves over to L.C.*)
SALLY: } MOTTY:	Aye.
JED:	Like to see your rooms now, folks ?
SALLY:	Yes, please. Come on, Percy. (*Moves towards porch*).
JED:	Oh, and Mr. Piggott. (*Doubtfully*). The gang having come into town for the celebration, I guess you'd like me to serve 'em a drink at the Lone Star ? (*Chorus cheer*).
MOTTY:	What, all of 'em ?
PERCY:	Aye !
SALLY:	Now, Dad, Percy mustn't be mean.

EXIT SALLY.

PERCY:	No, Motty, I mustn't be mean. (*To* JED). They've come specially to welcome me, and I'll show 'em my appreciation. Here, Mister, let's have a do, give 'em all lemonade.
MOTTY:	Percy Piggott you'll die in gutter. (*Exit into hotel with Sally*).
TEXANS:	Lemonade ! !

CALL: BUDDY AND LILAC

PERCY:	Go on, lemonade and make 'em big uns.

MUSIC CUE No. 2

" I'M SAVING UP FOR SALLY." 1 *Verse.* 1 *Refrain.*
2*nd Verse.* 2*nd Refrain.* 3*rd Refrain.*
No. 2. " SAVING UP FOR SALLY."
(PERCY AND CHORUS) *See Dance Plot.*

Verse 1.

PERCY:	I may seem rather careful, a little slow to spend

Don't often push the boat out and haven't brass
to lend
It's not that I'm a meany or spending comes amiss
In confidence I'll tell you, lads, the reasons for
it's this.

Refrain 1.

I'm saving up for Sally
Saving for a rainy day
I save what I can spare,
A penny here and there,
And just to keep us off the rocks
I pop it in me money box !
I'm not a lad to dally,
Of Sally I'm as proud as I can be !
It's a lovely thing to be her beau
But all the same I'd like to know
If Sally's saving up a bit for me !

Verse 2.

I haven't popped the question or asked her to be mine
But Sally's such a darling I'll have to toe the line
It may be any minute, I hope she'll say " I will "
But till I pluck me courage up I keep on saving still.

Refrain 2.

I'm saving up for Sally.
I'm saving for a honeymoon

CHORUS:	He's saving for a honeymoon.
PERCY:	I've got to buy a ring

A mattress with a spring
There's one thing I'll have to get
A nice new shiny bassinet

I'm not the lad to dally
    Of Sally I'm as proud as I can be
But before I go to that expense
    I'd like to know in self-defence
If Sally's saving up a bit for me !

Refrain 3.

CHORUS: He's saving up for Sally
    Saving up for a rainy day
He saves what he can spare
    A penny here and there,
And just to keep him off the rocks
He pops it in his money hox.

PERCY: Oh, I'm not the lad to dally
    Of Sally I'm as proud as I can be !
It's a lovely thing to be her beau
    But all the same I'd like to know
If Sally's saving up a bit for me !

CHORUS: If Sally's saving up a bit for him !

PERCY: Come on, folks, lemonade !

(*He exits into hotel followed by* TEXANS *shouting and cheering*)

MUSIC CUE No. 2A. *Fade out after exit.*

ENTER LILAC *and* BUDDY (*from back of Hotel through swing doors*) *who just see the tail end of the exit into bar. They look at each other and* BUDDY *brings down wicker chair from left of Hotel.*

LILAC: Did you see what he looked like ?

BUDDY: No, darn it. Just missed him. Maybe we can get him by himself later on ?

LILAC: Oh, Buddy, do you really think this Mr. Piggott might back our show ?

BUDDY: A guy who throws money around like water ? Sure it's in the bag. I can see it all. " Percival Piggott presents ' Garter Girl ' by Buddy Delany "—on Broadway . . . starring *you*. (*Sitting astride chair*).

LILAC: Me on Broadway ?

BUDDY: Sure ! Then we can get married—wait—(*closing his eyes*).

LILAC: What's the matter ?

BUDDY: I'm just looking at your name in lights.

LILAC: Hold it while I look at yours.

BUDDY: Better get your telescope, kid. They put authors very small.

LILAC: Gee, wouldn't it be wonderful ?

BUDDY:	Or would it ? Come to think of it, it's a great way of losing your girl.
LILAC:	Now Buddy ....
BUDDY:	What do *I* get when you belong to *Broadway* ?
LILAC:	*Me*, you big dope !
BUDDY:	(*Shaking his head*) Uh-huh. I'm not good at sharing.

SWITCHBOARD CUE No. 4.

MUSIC CUE No. 3 " THE THING ABOUT YOU."

LILAC:	I sometimes wonder how I could have been dumb enough to fall in love with you ! (*Kneeling on* BUDDY'S *R.*)
BUDDY:	(*Indignantly*) Is that so ?
LILAC:	Yes it is ... (*sings*) (*Giving her a lovable punch under chin*) ....

CALL: PERCY PIGGOTT.

DUET " THE THING ABOUT YOU "

(LILAC AND BUDDY) *See Dance Plot.*

1 *Pick up three bars intro.* 1 *Verse*, 1 *Refrain*, 2nd *Verse*, 2nd *Refrain.*

VERSE 1.

LILAC:	Have you ever contemplated, that you're kind of complicated,
BUDDY:	You think you're simple as a pie, well, I'm darned if I know just why,

REFRAIN 1.

BUDDY:	I'm a scatterbrain, I can't explain the thing about you. That certain strange exciting thing, that only you can claim.
LILAC:	Though you're quite a guy, I could never tie a string about you. You're bad as bad, then good as gold, and never you're twice the same.
BUDDY:	Words seem to fail me and I'm all at sea
LILAC:	There's no describing my favourite personality,
BUDDY:	It 'ud take too long to compose a song, to sing about you And so I guess I must confess, when all my thinking is through That the thing about you, Baby, is that you're you.

VERSE 2.

LILAC:	I seem to gather from that build up, I'm a form that can't be filled up ? known as ' X.'
BUDDY:	So what use breaking our necks ? You're the formula

REFRAIN 2

BUDDY: It's a level bet that I'll never get that thing about you.
That great infuriating charm, that knocks me off my feet.
Though I don't know much, there's a subtle touch of spring about you
Like some enchanted April day, you're stormy and then you're sweet.
No need to tell you how you get me down!
But you add up to the most attractive thing in town.
How could I define how this heart of mine goes " Zing " about you.
But wait a bit and I'll admit (and on my heart is my hand).
That the thing about you, Baby, is that you're grand.

LILAC: You're fine.

BUDDY: You're swell.

LILAC: You're mine.

BOTH: But I guess you're kind of hard to understand.

SWITCHBOARD CUE No. 5.

(LILAC *finishes on* BUDDY'S *knee at end of Duet*).
After BUDDY *and* LILAC'S *duet*, *ENTER* PERCY *from Hotel, dressed in cowboy chaps brandishing his revolvers.*

PERCY: Howdy, folks! Aren't you going in for some lemonade? It's mighty fine—mighty fine !

BUDDY: Thanks, I don't use it.

CALL: SALLY.

PERCY: (*To* LILAC) Oh, do have one, Miss. You can have a bun and all, if you like.

LILAC: (*Intrigued*) You don't say...a *whole* bun !

PERCY: (*Shyly*) You could have two buns if you wanted 'em.

BUDDY: (*Impatiently*) Come on Lilac (*They move over to L.*)

PERCY: (*Shyly*) I'm Percy Piggott—the millionaire !

BUDDY: You're Mr. Piggott the millionaire ? (*Turning and moving back slowly to* PERCY *followed by* LILAC).

PERCY: Aye—well I'm two-gun Piggott now !

LILAC: (*Slowly*) And you're going to give me *two* whole buns?

PERCY: Well, wait a minute—I was a bit rash when I said that. (*He puts his hand into R. hand pocket to check money*).

While PERCY *searches his pocket,* LILAC *signals violently to* BUDDY, *pointing to the script in his pocket.* BUDDY *doesn't get her at first, but finally does.*

PERCY: (*Having checked his money*) Yes, you can have two little 'uns.

BUDDY:	Mr. Piggott, I'd like to have a word with you. You don't know who I am. (*Crossing behind* PERCY *to his right and pulling him down stage R.*)
PERCY:	Oh, yes I do. You're the lawyer feller from New York.
BUDDY:	Wrong. This is Miss Lilac Delany, the musical comedy star.
LILAC:	Oh, how'd you do!
PERCY:	(*Impressed*) Go on! Pleased to meet you—Turned out nice again, hasn't it ?
BUDDY:	You've heard of her, of course.
PERCY:	No. Not in Newton-Le-Willows, we only have Mrs. Dale's Diary there !
BUDDY:	At the moment, she's studying her part in her next production.
LILAC:	It's called " The Garter Girl."

She holds out her hand behind PERCY'S *back, and* BUDDY *hands her the script.*

BUDDY:	(*Showing script*) Here's the script.
PERCY:	(*Gazing at script fascinated*)
BUDDY:	We can stage it tomorrow.
LILAC:	And what a story.

PERCY'S *head turns with each line.*

BUDDY:	New York, in the Naughty Nineties—
LILAC:	Glamour and glitter—
BUDDY:	Garters and Girls.
LILAC:	And I'm the Garter Girl.
BUDDY:	(*Reaching across* PERCY *and taking script*). Get this for her first entrance. Act One, Scene One, The Famous Astor Roof Garden—
LILAC:	A party's on—
BUDDY:	A posse of waiters carry on a gigantic pie. The crust is cut—and out jumps—
LILAC:	The Garter Girl—me ! (*Pirouetting over L. and holding up her skirt and showing her right leg*).
PERCY:	Do you come out of a pie ?
BUDDY: } LILAC: }	Out of a pie.
PERCY:	Well, I'll go to our 'ouse.
BUDDY: } LILAC: }	Pardon ?
PERCY:	I'd like to see you come out of a pie. (*To* LILAC).
BUDDY:	You *would* ? (*Twisting* PERCY *round and shaking hands*). Then it's settled.

PERCY:	What's settled ?
BUDDY:	We'll let you back the show.
LILAC:	It's the chance of a lifetime. (*She twists him round*).
BUDDY:	A hundred thousand dollars'll see it on.
LILAC:	And you might make a million. (*She twists him round again*).
PERCY:	But I've already *got* a million.
LILAC:	But that won't last for ever.

ENTER SALLY *in pretty dress from Hotel.*

SALLY:	Percy.
PERCY:	I'm a bit giddy!

He completely forgets the DELANYS, *to their exasperation.*

SALLY:	Who are these people ?
PERCY:	(*By way of introduction*). This feller's a theatrical, and this young woman's coming out of a pie.
SALLY:	Out of a pie ?
PERCY:	In her garters.
SALLY:	Percy!
BUDDY:	We've been telling Mr. Piggott of our forthcoming musical comedy production—
LILAC:	On Broadway, Honey. It'll knock 'em for a loop.
SALLY:	(*Enthusiastically*) How wonderful.
PERCY:	And they're going to let me give them the money to do it.
SALLY:	(*After a pause*) Oh. (*Going towards the hotel*) Father!
PERCY:	It's all right, Sally. Don't bother Motty. (*To* BUDDY) I'm sorry, young feller, but I don't think show business is quite in my line.
BUDDY:	Now just think it over, Mr. Piggott. You don't have to say " yes " right now.
LILAC:	Of course you don't.
BUDDY:	We'll come back in a few minutes. (*To* SALLY) Talk to your husband, Mrs. Piggott. I can see you're all for it.
LILAC:	(*Meeting* SALLY'S *eye*) H'm . . . Come on, Buddy.

(*They exit L.2.E.*)

SALLY:	What is all this " Mrs. Piggott " stuff ? People here do seem to jump to conclusions!
PERCY:	Well you're not worried, are you ?
SALLY:	(*Hastily changing subject*) Percy what's all this about putting cash into a show ? I've heard that's a certain way of losing money.

PERCY:	I'm not putting any money into a show—I've got something to *keep* my money for now!
SALLY:	Have you?

CALL: MR. CONNELLY.

PERCY:	(*After a shy pause*) You understand, don't you, Sally?
SALLY:	Percy, I don't see what *you* being a millionaire has got to do with *me*. I'm just an ordinary girl....

(*Sitting on stage R.C.*)
MUSIC CUE No. 4 "ORDINARY PEOPLE"

PERCY:	That's nowt to swank about! I'm just an ordinary chap!!

SWITCHBOARD CUE No. 6.

(*Sitting on stage L.C.*)
No. 4 "ORDINARY PEOPLE"

(PERCY and SALLY)
1 *Verse*, 1 *Refrain*, 2nd *Verse*, 2nd *Refrain and TAG*.
VERSE 1.

PERCY:	You know Sally when I was just a kid like all the others did I used to dream about my life's ambition. In turn I planned to be a sailor on the sea, A crook, a Boy Scout or even a politician! Yet here I am with all the dreams I've had, An ordinary chap—but still I'm glad...
SALLY:	Are you?

REFRAIN 1.

PERCY:	Ordinary people like you and me, Happy and contented as we can be, We can walk on air on our ordinary feet Strolling hand in hand along an ordinary street. Ordinary people we are until The ordinary time o' day is through When that ordinary moon is in the ordinary sky What extraordinary things we do!

VERSE 2.

SALLY:	I had my dreams as well, though they're not much to tell My schoolgirl head was filled with idle fancies And most of all by far I longed to be a star The heroine of Hollywood romances! But here I am, with nothing as I planned, An ordinary girl—and my! It's grand...

REFRAIN 2.

SALLY: with Vocal Background:	Ordinary people like you and me, Happy and contented as we can be, We can walk on air on our ordinary feet Strolling hand in hand along an ordinary street Ordinary people are we until The ordinary time o' day is through

PERCY SOLO:	And when the ordinary moon—is in the ordinary sky What extraordinary things we do.
CHORUS:	We do—
SALLY, PERCY, CHORUS:	What extraordinary things we do.

> NOTE: *Lights are checked for this number and stay down until end of scene; sunset effect on sky, lights in hotel, etc. CHORUS join in number from behind windows of hotel. They pull down the blinds of the hotel windows at end last note of number.*

PERCY:	(*His heart full*) Oh, Sally!
SALLY:	(*Changing subject*) Do you think you're goin' to like living here ?
PERCY:	Living here ? Not me, once I've seen lawyers we're all going back to Newton-Le-Willows.
SALLY:	Dad and I may be, but you've got a house here…
PERCY:	A house ? Since when ? I haven't been here five minutes. I've had my name down for four years at home and haven't got one yet!
SALLY:	It was your Uncle's and now (*Points to mansion*)… it belongs to you.
PERCY:	Is that mine? (*Looking over to house down L*) I don't half feel queer. Do you know, Sally, I've never *owned* anything all to myself before… and as soon as I've seen this lawyer, if everything's all right, I'm going to ask you something… (*He boggles*).
SALLY:	Are you ?
PERCY:	I am an' all !
SALLY:	(*Suddenly shy—grabbing his hand*) Come on, Percy. Let's go and look at it! (*They go over to house L.— PERCY sees bunch of cactus below door*).
PERCY:	By gum, I'm goin' to have one of them when they're ripe! Don't they grow big cucumbers here!
SALLY:	Let's knock.
PERCY:	(*Knocks on door*) Come on—let's run! (*They both run across stage to R.C.*)
SALLY:	But Percy—it's your house.

> *The broken door, which is hinged to the bottom sill, collapses straight on stage—a pause—then framed in the doorway is a figure (*CONNELLY *moves to stage over the fallen door*).*

CONNELLY:	Mr. Piggott ?
PERCY:	Aye.
CONNELLY:	(*Referring to paper*) Percival Gordon Kitchener Piggott?

B

PERCY:	Aye.
CONNELLY:	Born—
PERCY:	I think so !
CONNELLY:	—the 10th of June 1909 at 11 Albert Road, Newton-Le-Willows in the Duchy of Lancaster ?
PERCY:	If I wasn't, then my Mother has been telling stories.
CONNELLY:	Mr. Piggott, I'm glad to meet you. (*He shakes hands with* PERCY). I am George Connelly, representing your late Uncle's estate. I was just going over the house.
PERCY:	It looks as if it could do with a bit of going over. I'll get my bucket and wash leather out in the morning. Pleased to meet you, Mr. Connelly (*Shaking hands with* CONNELLY). This is Miss Whittle ... We know each other.
SALLY:	How do you do.
CONNELLY:	How do you do, young lady. (*He moves over to* SALLY *R.C. and shakes hands*). If you wouldn't mind leaving us for a moment ... ?
PERCY:	Oh no, I don't have any secrets from Sally, Mister !
CONNELLY:	Under the terms of your late Uncle's will, all I have to say must be said in *absolute privacy*. (*He moves over to L.C.*)
SALLY:	Of course, Percy—I understand perfectly, Mr. Connelly. (*Going up to porch*). I must go and see what's happened to Dad.
PERCY:	But don't be far away, Sally, 'cos when I've seen him I've got something to say to *you* in absolute privacy!
	With a happy wave EXIT SALLY *to Hotel.*
PERCY:	Isn't she lovely ?
CONNELLY:	(*Casually*) Very charming. (*Briskly*) Now, Mr. Piggott, let's get down to business ....
	(CONNELLY *sits on chair stage C.*)
PERCY:	(*Not attending*) I should have popped the question when I was in the mood! I'll have to work myself up all over again.
CONNELLY:	(*Sharply*) I must have your full attention, sir,
PERCY:	Yes, eh, oh yes! Sorry. You know how it is—when I'm with Sally—I get sort of carried away.
	(PERCY *brings down chair from stage R. and sits*)
CONNELLY:	Your uncle was a fabulously wealthy man. Do you appreciate ?
PERCY:	This is a snapshot of Sally and me when we were on holiday in Blackpool.
CONNELLY:	Do you appreciate that the estate left to you amounts to—

PERCY:	(*Dreamily looking at hotel*) I know, I know—a million dollars. That's the Blackpool Tower, and see them three donkeys ? Well we went riding on them. There was a big woman of eighteen stone got on the little one and it bent in the middle.
CONNELLY:	It's not *one* million, Mr. Piggott . . . *eight* million dollars.
PERCY:	Fancy eight million! (*Doing a " take "*) *What* ? . . . Eight million—but it *couldn't* . . .
CONNELLY:	Yes, sir. One million to be paid to you forthwith—
PERCY:	Forthwith—
CONNELLY:	—and a further seven million to be paid . . .
PERCY:	I know, withforth.
CONNELLY:	. . . when you have carried out the conditions of the will.
PERCY:	Conditions ? What conditions ? Oh so there's a catch in it, is there ?
CONNELLY:	There is! In order to inherit the full amount you have to spend one million dollars before the first of January next.
PERCY:	Spend one million in four months? Was my Uncle daft ?
CONNELLY:	No, but your uncle hated meanness, so he swore—
PERCY:	I bet he did. I would have done an' all.
CONNELLY:	—that he wouldn't leave his fortune to anyone who couldn't spend money.
PERCY:	Going a bit of a bust is one thing, but a million dollars in four months—only a Government could spend that. (*Shocked*)—it isn't *respectable*!
CONNELLY:	You can of course refuse the legacy . . . *(Rising and collecting brief case and hat which he put on floor when he sat in chair)*
PERCY:	(*Hastily*) Oh no, I didn't say that ! But how could I do it.
CONNELLY:	(*Putting hat and brief case on chair*) That is your problem ! Now— CALL: SINGERS, DANCERS, MOTTY, BUDDY, LILAC, JED, SALLY.
PERCY:	Somebody coming ?
CONNELLY:	(*Turning and looking up stage*)—as to the three minor conditions. One: the money must be spent, not *given* . . .
PERCY:	That's fair enough.
CONNELLY:	Two: you mustn't tell a living soul what you are attempting to do.
PERCY:	What, not tell *anyone* ? Not even Sally ?
CONNELLY:	No, sir. And, lastly, Clause Three: No matrimonial entanglements whatsoever.
PERCY:	What, no courting ? . . . Oh then in that case it's all off.
CONNELLY:	You really mean that ?

PERCY:	Yes, no courting!
CONNELLY:	(*Taking out a large wad of notes and flicking them to tempt* PERCY) Oh well, that's a pity because I had brought you a little *on account* ...
PERCY:	I dont' care what you've brought me—er—(*Seeing notes and doing a "take." Struggling*) Can I have a touch? (CONNELLY *gives him the notes,* PERCY *flicks them*) Eight million and no courting!! Oh—well? Oh, dear, but what about Sally, though?
CONNELLY:	If the lady really cares, believe me, Mr. Piggott, she'll wait. Or (*slyly*) perhaps you'd rather tell her that there's no inheritance after all.
	(*He takes notes back from* PERCY)
PERCY:	Well you see, it's very awkward—I'm half spoken for already.
	(CONNELLY *goes to put money back in his pocket*)
PERCY:	No, no, don't put it away! (*Taking money back*). I'll get over it some road!
PERCY:	You said I'd to spend it in four months—well I'll make it easy for myself—I'll spend it in four weeks.
CONNELLY:	My congratulations Mr. Piggott—and now, good evening, sir. (*Putting on hat and picking up brief case and moving over L.*)
PERCY:	Are you going?
CONNELLY:	Yes, I have my train to catch. Don't forget—four months. Remember the conditions, Mr. Piggott, and go right ahead. You have my address in New York. Goodbye and the best of luck. See you New Year's Eve. (*Exits L.2.E.*)

SWITCHBOARD CUE No. 7.

PERCY:	Happy New Year! ... Sally, Motty, where are you—
	ENTER SALLY *and* MOTTY *from hotel.*
	ENTER OTHERS from hotel—JED *and* CHORUS.
MOTTY:	What's to do?
SALLY:	Percy!
SALLY:	Has he gone?
PERCY:	Aye.
MOTTY:	Was it all right? Do you get the money?
PERCY:	Yes (*Holding up wad*). Look!
MOTTY:	Jumping Jehoshaphat! (*Stares at money*) Here, you'd best let me look after that for you.
SALLY:	(*Breaking in*) Be quiet, Dad. Leave Percy alone. He's got something to tell me ...
MOTTY:	What's he got to tell *you*?

SALLY:	Well, can't you guess ?
JED:	Sure, I get it. Come on, you guys.
MOTTY:	Oh, I see what you mean.

They start to move away up stage.

PERCY:	(*Desperately*) No—no, come back, everybody, you mustn't leave me!
SALLY:	(*Hurt*) But, Percy—! You said—!
PERCY:	I know I did, I was here when I said it, wasn't I ? But you see it's a bit funny now!
SALLY: } MOTTY: }	Funny ?
PERCY:	Well, it's a bit awkward—er—I mean—there's a lot of business.
MOTTY: } SALLY: }	Business ?
SALLY:	(*Puzzled*) Business ? I don't understand.
PERCY:	I can't explain, love, but when a man comes into money —well, things sort of *happen*!
SALLY:	(*Emotionally*) Of course. I'm sure you must be very busy now! (*Walks away to R.C.*)
PERCY:	Oh, Sally—! It's one of the conditions.
MOTTY:	Conditions ? What are you talking about ?
PERCY:	He said it was going to be difficult. (*Sees* JED *waiting with his hand out*). What do *you* want ?
JED:	A little matter of sixteen and a half bucks...
PERCY:	Sixteen and a half bucks ? What for ?
JED:	The lemonade!
PERCY:	Lemonade be damned—give 'em all champagne.
TEXANS:	Champagne!

Cheers from TEXANS.

JED:	Yes *sir*!

JED hurries joyfully into saloon, followed by SERVANTS. *ENTER* LILAC *and* BUDDY. *L.2.E.*

MOTTY:	Champagne! (*Horrified*). Percy Piggott, have you gone daft ?
PERCY:	No, I haven't, but I've started, I've got money now, and I'm going to do things in style.
LILAC:	Three cheers for Percy Rockefeller.

She pats PERCY *on back, which* SALLY *doesn't much like.*

PERCY: } TEXANS: }	Hip, hip, oh (*Once*).
LILAC: } BUDDY: }	Hip, Hip Hooray (*Three times*).
MOTTY:	Who's this ?

PERCY:	Miss Lilac Delany, the actress. I'm going to back her show.
BUDDY:	Do you really mean it?
PERCY:	I don't tell lies.
LILAC:	(*Astonished and delighted and throwing her arms around* PERCY) You lovely great hunk of man!
BUDDY:	(*Earnestly*) Brother, you won't regret it.
MOTTY:	Back her show? What show?
PERCY:	It's all about a pie; with women rushing in and out in their garters.
SALLY:	(*Shocked*) Percy!
MOTTY:	(*Firmly*) You'll back no show. You'll lose every penny you've got.
PERCY:	That's my business.
MOTTY:	Percy Piggott, have you gone stark staring mad?
PERCY:	No, but I've started. (*To* LILAC) Here's a month's salary in advance. (*Hands her a handful of bills*).
LILAC:	Catch me, Buddy. (*She falls backward into* BUDDY's *arms*).
PERCY:	And here's a month's salary in advance for you. (*Thrusts bills into his hand*).
BUDDY:	(*Protesting*) But, listen—
PERCY:	(*Severely*) Now, now, no backing out.
LILAC:	No backing out!! We're going to pack! Come on Buddy.
BUDDY:	But Mr. Piggott (LILAC *drags* BUDDY *off R. below hotel*).
MOTTY:	(*Eyeing the distribution of bills to actors*) Well, I've never acted, but I can try. (*Holds out hand*).
PERCY:	(*Firmly*) Not in my show. You're manager of the firm.
MOTTY:	What firm?
PERCY:	The Percy Piggott's Window Cleaning Corporation. (*Stuffs bills into his hand*). We'll buy some buckets in the morning. Here's a month's wages in advance. And, Sally, you're the secretary—(*Holding out wad of bills*). Here's two months' wages in advance for you.
SALLY:	No, thank you.
PERCY:	But, Sally, I must have a secretary and someone to look after me.
SALLY:	(*Looking at* LILAC) I'm sure you'll find plenty of people to do that. (*Turning to* MOTTY) Daddy, take me away.
MOTTY:	Don't worry, lass. He's not himself. It's not Percy Piggott talking—it's the lemonade. (MOTTY *leads* SALLY *up to hotel where they exit*).
PERCY:	Oh, is it! Bring on that champagne.

(JED *and man bring on two magnums of champagne.*
JED *pours into* TEXAN'S *glass*).
Eh, eh, me first—I'm paying for it. (JED *fills his mug*).

JED: C'mon folks, up with yer glasses, to Percy-Val Piggott—
The biggest hell raiser of them all. (JED *bangs* PERCY
on the back).

All cheer and drink.

MUSIC CUE No. 5

CALL: PAULA, MANICURIST, SHOESHINE BOY,
   HEAD ATTENDANT, BUDDY, SALLY,
   HAIRDRESSER.

No. 5 " ZIP GOES A MILLION "
(PERCY *and* CHORUS)
1 *Refrain*, 1 *Verse*, 2nd *Refrain*.

REFRAIN 1.

PERCY: Zip goes a million
      It's a great sensation
   Keeping cash in
      Circulation!
   I'm not saving up
      Like Tom, Dick and Hank,
   Got no money
      Wasting time in the bank.

                    (*Tabs close behind* CHORUS)
   Zip goes a million
      Going to start a party,
   Dish the dollars
      Like a clown
   Easy come and easy go—don't be dumb
      And spend all your dough
   Zip goes a million—and a million million
      Percy Piggott's in town.

VERSE 1.

PERCY: When you fall for someone sweet and give your heart
         away
   Every single time you meet it's window shopping day
   Diamond bracelet, coat of mink, the biggest car they've
         got
   You go crazy and you think you'd like to buy the lot!

REFRAIN 2.

ALL: Zip goes a million
      It's a great sensation
   Keeping cash in
      Circulation
   I'm not saving up like Tom, Dick or Hank
   Got no money—wasting in the bank
   Zip goes a million—goin' to start a party
   Dish the dollars like a clown

PERCY:	Easy come and easy go
	Don't be dumb—but spend all your dough
CHORUS:	Zip goes a million—and a million million
PERCY:	Two Gun Piggott's in town.

At end of number PERCY *draws two pistols from his hips and fires into the air.*

SWICHBOARD CUE No. 8.

BLACK OUT.

MUSIC CUE No. 5A, SEGUE...

" I'M SAVING UP FOR SALLY "

SWITCHBOARD CUE No. 9.

ACT 1

SCENE 2 (Playing Time: 7 mins.)

THE RITZ CARLTON HOTEL, NEW YORK
MANICURIST'S PARLOUR, WITH SHOESHINE CHAIR
ADJACENT.

Characters in this scene:

PAULA
HEAD ATTENDANT
MANICURIST
BUDDY
SHOESHINE BOY
SALLY
HAIRDRESSER

As swags open music fades.

A MANICURIST is attending to Paula Van Norden
THE HEAD ATTENDANT (a sort of supervisor) is
nearby, glancing at a periodical.

The SHOESHINE BOY is squatting by his chair, reading a tabloid.

HEAD BARBER also is reading.

HEAD ATTENDANT:	Why here's a picture of you, Miss Van Norden, next to Percy Piggott.
PAULA:	Who, for Heaven's sake is Percy Piggott ?
HEAD ATTENDANT:	You don't know ? He's front page news, Miss Van Norden.
MANICURIST:	I'll say! He's just come into a Million Dollars, and they say he isn't married. He's all alone. His Secretary, Miss Whittle, comes in here for a hair-do.
PAULA:	Secretary! I thought you said he was alone.
HEAD ATTENDANT:	Oh there's nothing like that. Miss Whittle's a sweet girl.
PAULA:	She should be, with a million dollars' worth of sugar. (*Girls exchange glances*).

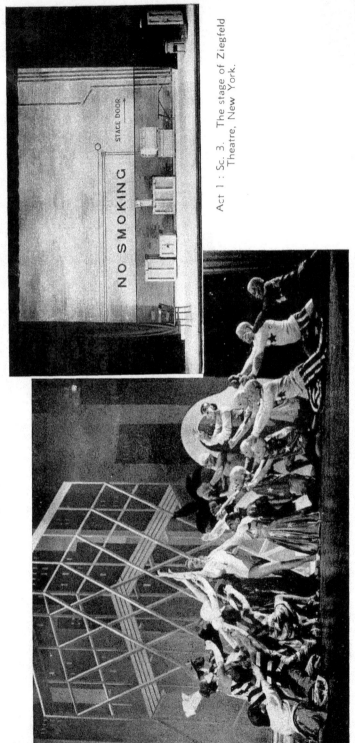

Act 1 : Sc. 3.   The stage of Ziegfeld Theatre, New York.

Finale to the rehearsal of 'The Story of Chiquita.'

Act 1 : Sc. 3.

THE HOLD-UP.　　　Act 1 : Sc. 4.

AN ALLEY OUTSIDE THE THEATRE
Door to be practical.

' Percy,' and ' Sally ' feature "Ordinary
People."　　Act 1: Sc. 4.

Act 1 : Sc. 4.

MANICURIST:	O.K. Miss Van Norden. (*P. Rises*).
PAULA:	(*Casually*) Where did you say he has his new offices?
HEAD ATTENDANT:	Mr. Piggott ? In the Rockefeller Plaza—and the parties he gives. Everybody who's anybody goes to them.
PAULA:	Then I expect we shall meet. In fact I'm sure we shall. Good afternoon. (*Tips* MANICURIST).
BOTH GIRLS:	Good afternoon, Miss Van Norden. (PAULA *exits R.*)
MANICURIST:	Gee! A quarter!! What a stinker.
HEAD ATTENDANT:	(*Shocked*) Shirley, Perleese! Her Father's a banker.
MANICURIST:	And what kind of a Banker! My dad says Old Man Van Norden ought to be in jail.

(Exit MANICURIST R. with tray)

ENTER BUDDY L.

BARBER:	Good afternoon, Mr. Delany, haircut ? (*Rising from stool*).
BUDDY:	(*To* BARBER *who is looking at him expectantly*) Not today, Johnny. Just a shine.
	He picks up a newspaper and sits on the shine-chair.
	The SHOESHINE BOY *gets busy on his shoes.*
BARBER:	I've just been reading about your play.
BUDDY:	(*Reading paper and not inclined for conversation*) Really ?
BARBER:	And how Mr. Piggott's going to spend all that money on it.
BUDDY:	Really ?
BARBER:	And his star, Miss Lilac Lamore. She looks lovely.
BUDDY:	She is—isn't she !
SHOESHINE:	She's new, isn't she ? How's she coming on ?
BUDDY:	Miss Lilac 'Lamore' is doing great!
BARBER:	It says here how he discovered her. Oh boy, he must be quite a picker.
BUDDY:	(*To shoeshine boy, shortly*) Get busy, Henry, I'm in a hurry. (*He buries himself behind his ⌐paper*).
SHOESHINE:	I'm gettin' busy, Mr. Delany.
	HEAD ASSISTANT *makes a face at the* MANICURIST *in acknowledgment of the snub.*
	ENTER SALLY R. *followed by* MANICURIST.
HEAD ASSISTANT:	Good afternoon, Miss Whittle.
MANICURIST:	Manicure, Miss Whittle.
SALLY:	I haven't time, just a jar of foundation cream, please. (MANICURIST *exits R.*)

HEAD ATTENDANT:	It must be wonderful to be private secretary to such an important person like Percy Piggott. He had his hair cut twice yesterday, and eight shampoos all in a row!
SALLY:	(*Bored*) Fancy that! (*Shoeshine boy exits L. with footstool*).
HEAD ASSISTANT:	You'd think he was just trying to get rid of his money.
SALLY:	Or his hair . . . (*Flaring up*). I wish you wouldn't keep talking about Mr. Piggott. Oh, I'm sorry but nobody ever seems to talk to me of anything else. (SALLY *sits on chair*). BUDDY, *hearing* SALLY'S *voice, lowers his paper.*
HEAD ASSISTANT:	Sorry, Miss Whittle. (*She exits R.I.E. taking her stool and paper*).
BUDDY:	(*Loudly*) We-ll now! I wonder who *that* can be over there ? (BARBER *exits L. with stool*).
SALLY:	(*Startled*) Who's that ?
BUDDY:	The name is Delany, ma'am . . .
SALLY:	(*Joyfully*) Buddy!
BUDDY:	Hi, Sally!
SALLY:	(*To Buddy—half-scared*) I say, did you hear what I said ?
BUDDY:	I did, and it goes for me, too, honey. Gee there are times when I'd like to get a crack at that nut.
SALLY:	'You should be pleased. After all he *is* making Lilac into a Broadway star. (SALLY *rises*).
BUDDY:	Sure, I know. But does she have to drag him around wherever she goes. Oh sorry Sally, but it just burns me up. (BUDDY *rises*).
SALLY:	I thought once he was going to say something . . . You know how you think . . . but he never *has*. (*Rising and moving L.*) I suppose I must have got it all wrong . . . I can't blame *him* can I ?
BUDDY:	We can't blame anybody—

MUSIC CUE No. 6. "IT TAKES NO TIME."

—but we can't help remembering.

SALLY:	(*With a sigh*) It's so difficult to forget.

" IT TAKES NO TIME TO FALL IN LOVE "
(SALLY, BUDDY AND SEXTETTE)
1 *Refrain*, 1 *Verse*, 2nd *Refrain.*
REFRAIN 1.

BUDDY:	It takes no time to fall in love No time at all to fall in love (*Three female singers enter Stage L. Three male singers enter Stage R.*)

SALLY:	One moment you may be so fancy free—so clever
BUDDY:	And then you find your peace of mind has gone for ever!
SALLY:	It takes no time to say " Hello " The only word you seem to know!

CALL: EDDIE, DANCERS, BUDDY, MOTTY, VAN NORDEN, SCENE SHIFTERS, PIANIST, LILAC.

BUDDY:	And from the very start—your happy heart— Goes flutt'ring like a dove!
SALLY: BUDDY: }	It takes no time at all to fall in love.

SWAGS CLOSE.

VERSE 1.

SALLY:	Can't think how it happened Oh, but it surprised me. No one had advised me what to do.
BUDDY:	Can't think how it happened! Sweet, but kind of frightened Like the summer lightning from the blue.
SALLY:	Just a chap in a cap On a street in the rain
BUDDY:	Just the ghost of a smile From a girl in a train
BOTH:	And it's something your heart can't explain.

CALL: PERCY, PAULA, DRESS DESIGNER, MUSICAL DIRECTOR, SCENIC DESIGNER.

REFRAIN 2.

SEXTETTE VOCAL BACK-GROUND {

SALLY:	It takes no time to fall in love
BUDDY:	No time at all to fall in love
SALLY:	One moment you can be so fancy free—so clever
BUDDY:	And then you find your peace of mind has gone forever!
SALLY:	It takes no time to say " Hello " The only word you seem to know!
BUDDY:	And from the very start—your happy heart— Goes flutt'ring like a dove!

(SEXTETTE *exit*. MEN *R*. GIRLS *L*.)

BUDDY & SALLY:	It takes no time at all to fall in love.

SALLY *exits L*. BUDDY *exits R*.
SWITCHBOARD CUE No. 10.

BLACK OUT AT END OF NUMBER.

MUSIC SEGUE TO No. 7. "PIANO BALLET."

Orchestra fades out as piano starts on stage.

ACT 1
SCENE 3 (Playing Time: 16 mins.)
THE STAGE OF THE ZIEGFELD THEATRE. EVENING.
SWITCHBOARD CUE No. 11.

Characters in this scene:
EDDIE
BUDDY
LILAC
PERCY
PAULA
VAN NORDEN
MOTTY
DRESS DESIGNER
SCENE DESIGNER
MUSICAL DIRECTOR
REHEARSAL PIANIST - TWO SCENE SHIFTERS
DANCERS

EDDIE: (*Shouting*) Tabs!! (*Tabs open after 4 bars music*).

The stage is cleared. A rehearsal is in progress, with piano player. In balletic form, EDDIE, the producer, is taking the DANCERS through a routine. The GIRLS are in very simple but cute " Sloppy Joe" practice uniform with the initials " P.P." on them.

No. 7 REHEARSAL BALLET.

MUSIC CUE

One, two, three, and— *Piano on stage starts.*
(*After 14 bars piano music*)

EDDIE: (*Clapping hands*) Stop, Betsy Lou, you're late on that beat again! What do you girls think you are? Performing elephants?

GIRL: The girls are tired, Eddie!

EDDIE: So we're tired, I'm tired—what else do you expect when we rehearse day and night for eight weeks!!

GIRL: Well, maybe a short break then?

EDDIE: O.K. Five minutes—

(*Girls disperse and relax up stage*)
ENTER BUDDY briskly from R.2.E. He is production manager of the show. Background of " atmosphere," 2 STAGE HANDS moving flat from Stage R. and setting it in front of 2nd Red Leg—Stage L.

BUDDY: Evening, kids. Evening, Eddie.

ALL: Good evening, Mr. Delany!

BUDDY:	Lilac around ?
EDDIE:	In her dressing room. Some packages came for her.
A.S.M.:	Call Miss Lamore, somebody.
VOICES:	Miss Lamore; wanted on stage. (Etc.)
BUDDY:	(*Scornfully*) Lilac ' Lamore '—when she joined my act her name was Nellie Crumb. Has Mr. Piggott been around yet ?
EDDIE:	Not yet.
BUDDY:	How's every little thing ? Well up to schedule ?
EDDIE:	(*Bitterly*) Anything funny you've got to say, you put in your script. Up to *schedule*! I'm all behind. This show will never be ready.
BUDDY:	Well, what's wrong now ?
EDDIE:	Piggott makes me work on a new number every day.

ENTER LILAC *proudly in fur coat from R.3.E.*

LILAC:	Was somebody asking for me ?
DANCERS:	Holy Smoke. Ooh! Get that! (*Admiring coat*) Who's my Daddy now ? What is it, rat skin ? (Etc.)
BUDDY:	Indian summer, eh! Kinda hot for a fur coat, isn't it, Doll!
LILAC:	Not for a fur coat as hot as *this*.
BUDDY:	Well, you look George all the way! (*To Eddie*) Blue mink—who ordered blue mink ?
LILAC:	(*Airily*) Oh, I don't know, I guess it must have been Percy P. His card was with it.
BUDDY:	You mean the coat's not for the show—that it's a *gift* from him to *you* ?
LILAC:	Gosh sakes! (*Offended*) Can't a gentleman give a lady a little souvenir without everybody acting as though she'd *stolen* it ?
EDDIE:	(*To* PIANIST) O.K. Jake, we'll take that number now. Clear everybody!
BUDDY:	So that's it. (*To* LILAC *who has started a tap practice*). I guess you think you're doing *great*. (*Roughly turning to him*).
LILAC:	You quit the act.
BUDDY:	So—I quit the act.
LILAC:	Well, what are you beefing about? You said you wanted me to get *right to the top*!
BUDDY:	Yeah—but I didn't say *how*!
LILAC:	I resent that! Mr. Piggott is a gentleman!
BUDDY:	Sure. From the word " stop."
LILAC:	Well, what do you know about *that* ?

EDDIE:	Break it up. (*Getting between* LILAC *and* BUDDY) Lilac, go and get changed.
LILAC:	I've been insulted.
EDDIE:	Get going, you've been insulted before.
LILAC:	Yes, but never by an—*author*.
	Exit R.2.E.
BUDDY:	(*To* EDDIE *furiously*) You hear that? She called me an author.
EDDIE:	Well, get off the stage and I'll keep your secret— (*Pushing* BUDDY *over to stage L.*)
BUDDY:	I wrote this show.
EDDIE:	But don't tell anybody. (BUDDY *exits L.2.E.*) (*To* DANCERS) Okay, kids. We'll take that routine again— (STAGE HANDS *run on flat from stage L. and set it in front of red legs stage R.*) (DANCERS *return to positions*)
BUDDY:	And let's get it right this time. One, two, three and (*To* PIANIST) Let her go.
	Music begins and dance—during which MOTTY *and* JAMES VAN NORDEN *infiltrate through the dancers from back stage right, causing a certain amount of dislocation.*
MOTTY:	It's a right biggun, an 'all, and it stretches from there to there. (*Looking into flys, and pointing from L. to R.*)
EDDIE:	Hold it!
	Piano and Dancing stops. MOTTY *and* VAN NORDEN *extricate themselves and come downstage.*
EDDIE:	(*Icily polite*) Good evening, gentlemen—more authors?
MOTTY:	I'm just showing a friend of Percy's around. This is Mr. Van Norden. Aye it's a right biggun! It's got a row of little bobbles on it!
EDDIE:	That's fine. (*Loudly and rudely*) Then get to hell out of it! Stand over there!
	Points to proscenium L. MOTTY *and* VAN NORDEN *go there obediently.*
MOTTY:	You know (*to* Van Norden) if I had him in Newton-Le-Willows . . .
EDDIE:	(*Fiercely*) Dont talk! (MOTTY *subsides*). Start again. One-and-two-and . . .
	Music starts at same spot as before: the routine is interrupted. PERCY *and* PAULA VAN NORDEN *ENTER in tuxedo and glamorous evening dress, back stage R. Before they can become entangled with the dancers,* EDDIE *claps his hands.*

PERCY:	It's a right biggun an' all.
EDDIE:	Hold it, everyone, hold it!

Piano and dancing peter out.

PERCY:	You see we got it over there, a right biggun! And it stretches from there to there (*looking into flys and pointing from L. to R.*) It's got a row of little bobbles on it!
EDDIE:	Good evening, Mr. Piggott.
PERCY:	Good evening, Eddie—Good evening, Girls.
DANCERS:	Good evening, Mr. Piggott.
PERCY:	(*To* EDDIE) I've brought a couple of friends of mine to have a peep at show.
EDDIE:	Sure, Mr. Piggott. (*To* PAULA) I'm afraid things are pretty rough just yet . . . we're still busy licking it into shape.

(*The two* SCENE SHIFTERS *take off* piano *R.2.E.*)

VAN NORDEN:	(*Pompously*) A peep behind the scenes is new and interesting to us from the outside world. (*Eyes* DANCERS *thoughtfully*).
PAULA:	(*Insincerely*) It's all too intriguing, Percy—I don't know how you do it—and I'm so proud of you.
PERCY:	Oh, I don't know—there's really nothing to it.

(*The* GIRLS *exit R. and L. entrances*)

ENTER DRESS DESIGNER *and* SCENE DE-SIGNER *R.2.E.*)

PAULA:	I'm going to tell hundreds of my most intimate friends all about the show and—

DRESS DESIGNER *hands material to* EDDIE.

EDDIE:	Excuse me, Mr. Piggott, would you Okay this ? (*Holds out material*).
PERCY:	What's this ?
EDDIE:	The material for the finale costumes, Mr. Piggott—imitation silver.
PERCY:	Imitation silver—I want gold, and *real* gold! No imitations for me. (EDDIE *gives material back to* DRESS DESIGNER *who exits R.2.E.*)
MOTTY:	But gold frocks for these girls'll cost thousands.
PERCY:	There won't be that much of 'em. (*To* EDDIE) I'll see some diamond necklaces in the morning.
EDDIE:	(*Overwhelmed*) S-sure, Mr. Piggott.
MOTTY:	Can't they go on the stage without diamond necklaces?
PERCY:	And catch their death of cold ?

(SCENE DESIGNER *hands* EDDIE *a sketch of a set*)

EDDIE:	Drawing for the Cuban Scene, P.P.
PERCY:	(*Studying drawing*) No, no, it's got to be bigger than that ... we've got to have it right round the back of the stage, with Nelson's Column in the middle.
EDDIE:	But P.P., the place isn't big enough for that.
	(EDDIE *gives back sketch to* SCENE DESIGNER *who exits R.2.E.*)
PERCY:	Not big enough? Then push out some of the walls ... Are those all the girls we've got?
EDDIE:	It's what you ordered, Sir.
PERCY:	Well, I want fifty more!
EDDIE:	But there won't be room for them on the stage.
PERCY:	Then let 'em sit in the stalls.
MOTTY:	But those are ten dollars each.
PERCY:	Good. Charge 'em up to me.
	MUSICAL DIRECTOR *has come on from R.2.E.*
MUSIC D.:	Orchestra's all okay. Makes a nice-a noice. Twenty-six of 'em.
PERCY:	Have you gone daft? What do you do?
MUSIC D.:	I makka de conduct (*waving his arms as though conducting an orchestra*).
PERCY:	(*Imitating him*) You makka de conduct! Well I want a hundred musicians down there and two to makka de conduct—one on each side!
MUSIC D.:	(*In Latin despair*) A hundred musicians ... but the orchestra pit isn't big enough. (*Gesture to orchestra pit*).
	CALL: SINGERS AND DANCERS.
PERCY:	Then tell 'em to dig pit deeper.
	(*M.D. exits R.2.R.*)
MOTTY:	Are you aware, Mr. Percival Piggott, that this show is costing two hundred thousand dollars already?
PERCY:	*Two* hundred? Two hundred—you've been at it again! Skin Flint! (*Accusingly*) You promised me *three*! What have you done with money?
MOTTY:	We've managed to save you a few thousand here and there.
PERCY:	(*In a thunderous voice*) Then don't do it again, understand that?—All of you!
EDDIE:	(*Cowed*) Yes, Mr. Piggott.
PERCY:	If I say " Spend three hundred thousand dollars " you spend it. I can't afford to put on a cheap show.
MOTTY:	Cheap show! (*He exits L.2.E.*)
PERCY:	Well, that's that. (*To* VAN NORDEN) You see what I'm up against? They never do anything you tell them.
	(EDDIE *sits astride chair R. reading music manuscript*).

VAN NORDEN:	They haven't your foresight—your breadth of view. They think in pennies while you dream in dollars. (*To* PAULA) What do you say, my dear ?
PAULA:	I think he spends far too much time over silly details. You look tired, Percy.
PERCY:	Aye, I do feel a bit done up.
PAULA:	Father was saying only this evening that you should get away from New York for a bit.
VAN NORDEN:	Absolutely essential. My yacht " Pleasure Cruise " is anchored off Sheep's Head Bay ...
PERCY:	Do you think I ought to go boating ?
PAULA:	Yachting, dear. But Percy, you should have a yacht *of your own.* A man in your social position needs an escape from city life.

(ENTER MOTTY L.2.E. Listening to a dialogue about the yacht)

PERCY:	I never thought of that ... a yacht.
VAN NORDEN:	In another minute, Percy, you'll be persuading me to part with the " Pleasure Cruise."
PERCY:	A yacht, eh ? Oh, I fancy myself on a yacht.
MOTTY:	(*To* VAN NORDEN) If he wants to go on t'water, he can ride on the ferry.
PERCY:	Shut up, Motty. (MOTTY *exits R.2.E.*) (*To* VAN NORDEN) Is it expensive ?
PAULA:	You two men talk it over right away. (*She moves over to stage R.*)

ENTER LILAC R.3.E.

LILAC:	Oh, Mr. Piggott! I really must thank you for this cute, adorable little fur coat.
PERCY:	Oh it's nothing really! It's only something a couple of my ferrets picked up. Meet two pals of mine—Mr. Van Norden and Miss Paula Van Norden—Lilac Lamore.
LILAC:	How do you do ? Isn't this (*showing off coat*) just the darlingest little number ?
PERCY:	Well, we can't have our star walking around in rags, you know!
PAULA:	(*Cats*) (*Moving to* LILAC *L.C.*) Congratulations, Miss Lamore. I know what a girl has to do to get a little mink ...
PERCY:	Aye, aye, they're off at Stockton!! (*Doing a comedy trot*).
LILAC:	Ah, and what has a girl got to do to get a little mink?
PAULA:	What minks do!
LILAC:	That has all the earmarks of a dirty crack.
PAULA:	(*Sneering*) I seem to have hit the nail on the head. (*Moving in front of* LILAC *to stage L. on* VAN NORDEN'S *R.*)

C

LILAC:	(*Belligerently*) Sister, the hitting on the head is about to begin . . . (*Making as though she is going to hit* PAULA *on the head*).
	PERCY *and* VAN NORDEN *get between* LILAC *and* PAULA.
PERCY:	Now, now, don't upset yourself.
VAN NORDEN:	Now, Paula, my dear, don't make a scene! (*Stepping in between* PAULA *and* LILAC).
PERCY:	Eeh, Lilac, don't be upset.
LILAC:	If you think I'm going to stand here and be high-hatted by that Society alley cat . . .
PAULA:	Alley cat.

CALL: POLICEMAN, BUDDY, LEFTY,
       TOUCH, MOTTY, PERCY, SALLY

LILAC:	Yes, alley cat?
PERCY:	Now, now, what are you worrying about alley cats for! They're lovely little things—you've only to stroke 'em like that and they go purr!
EDDIE:	(*Butting in*) Break this up people—I need the stage.
PERCY:	You need the stage (*Shaking* EDDIE'S *hand*), thanks a lot Eddie—your salary's up a thousand.
EDDIE:	Thanks. I'll put it on Lilac when the fight comes off. Clear please—and let's do the number.
PERCY:	Come on, Paula. I'll take you out front to watch.
	(PAULA *and* VAN NORDEN *exit L.2.E.*)
LILAC:	And keep her quiet. It's my big number.
PERCY:	Champion, love. And if it isn't big *enough*, you just let me know and I'll order a bigger one for you! (PERCY *exits L.2.E.*) (LILAC *furiously walks up and down stage twice then takes castanets from* EDDIE).
EDDIE:	(*Shouting*) Stand by to drop in the cloth. And if you don't mind, Miss Lamore, would you ease yourself out of that Park Avenue skunk? (LILAC *takes off fur coat and throws it at* EDDIE). Don't hurry, anyone. We might save somebody some money—and that would be just too bad!
	(EDDIE *exits R.2.E. taking chair and coat with him*)

MUSIC CUE No. 8 " CHIQUITA "

(LILAC & SEXTETTE & DANCERS)
SWITCHBOARD CUE No. 12.

LILAC:	In Seville there lived a dancer
	    And Chiquita was her name.
	Gee! That dancer knew the answer
	    Every movement in the game,

CALL: POLICEMAN, BUDDY, MOTTY,
       LEFTY, TOUCH, PERCY, SALLY

Her bolero, fandango,
Cachuca and tango
Were sultry and hot as a flame.

(SCENE 3A BACKCLOTH DROPS IN)

SEXTETTE: Ay-yi! ... Ay-yi!
(*In Pit*) They were sultry and hot as a flame.

LILAC: When she'd saved a lot of dough up
(Cause she knew pesetas talk)
She decided that she'd throw up
And take over to New York
Her bolero, fandango,
Cachuca and tango,
To the Copacabana and Stork

SEXTETTE: Ay-yi! ... Ay-yi!
(*In Pit*) To the Copacabana and Stork!

MAN SINGER: Through the Customs she went tearin'
(*Through* She was greeted with a grin.
Mike Prompt She'd no trouble in declarin'
Corner) She had only to begin
Her bolera, fandango,
Cachuca and tango,

SWITCHBOARD CUE No. 13.

The fellers said " Lady, you're in! Right in!"

16 *Bars Orchestra only for* LILAC'S *Dance.*

MAN SINGER: No, she'd never heard of Boogie up in Harlem.
(*Through* Over Chinatown her mind was just a blur.
Mike Prompt She was there to give New York a Spanish lesson
Corner) And by golly, here's what New York did to *her!*

DANCE. CHIQUITA BALLET.

AT END OF DANCE BLACK OUT. DRAW TABS.
SCENE 4 CLOTH DROP IN BEHIND.
DURING BALLET, SWITCHBOARD CUES
FOLLOW ON Nos. 14, 15, 16, 17, 18, 19, 20.
BLACKOUT ON CUE No. 21.
MUSIC CUE SEGUE. No. 9:

" NOTHING BREAKS BUT THE HEART "
TABS OPEN AS SOON AS CLOTH IS DOWN.

ACT 1
SCENE 4 (Playing Time: 12 mins.)
AN ALLEY OUTSIDE. EVENING.
SWITCHBOARD CUE No. 22.

Characters in this scene:

POLICEMEN	TOUCH
BUDDY	PERCY
MOTTY	SALLY
LEFTY	

Dark frame cloth downstage of an alley outside theatre with overhead light that gives it a deserted air. L.C. a steel pass door, L.C. a fire escape. R. and L. playbills of " GARTER GIRL " with luscious picture of LILAC DELANY and words " In Preparation." Outside door a long crate that has evidently been unpacked. MUSIC (intro. to No. 9). ENTER L TWO COPS strolling along swinging their sticks and looking up at playbill. They walk from Stage L. and exit Stage R. ENTER from Stage R. BUDDY. He looks harassed and stops to light a cigarette. Looks up at the playbill then throws down his cigarette and crushes it.

No. 9: " NOTHING BREAKS BUT THE HEART "
(BUDDY *and* SINGING SEXTETTE—*through mike in pit*)
1 *Refrain*, 1 *Verse*, 2*nd Refrain*.

REFRAIN 1.

BUDDY: Nothing breaks ... nothing breaks but the heart
                 When the love of your life is away, you're alone
                     and apart
            Then the ev'ning begins and the lamps start to glitter
                     and glow
                 There's the whole of the town at your feet—but
                     you've nowhere to go!
            No romance ... not a table for two.
                 There's a guy with a girl in the dark—but the guy
                     isn't you.
            As the stars tumble down and you wait for the dull day
                     to start,
                 When the love of your life is away . . . nothing
                     breaks but the heart.

VERSE 1.

BUDDY WITH   Then you hate the sound of the city
SEXTETTE   And the distant song of the street
VOCAL BACK- And you envy the laughter of lovers
GROUND IN   Going somewhere—with someone to meet
PIT: But for you no step on the stairway
                 Nor an eager voice on the phone
             And the pitiless clock seems to whisper
                 " You're alone, empty heart, all alone."

REFRAIN 2.

BUDDY   Nothing breaks ... nothing breaks but the heart
SINGING   When the love of your life is away, you're alone
(*Sextette*   and apart ...
harmonise When the ev'ning begins and the lamps start to glitter
all through   and glow
Chorus)   There's the whole of the town at your feet—but you've
                     nowhere to go
             No romance ... not a table for two.

> There's a guy with a girl in the dark—but the guy
> isn't you
> As the stars tumble down and you wait for the dull
> day to start
> When the love of your life is away, nothing breaks
> but the heart!

BUDDY *exits R.1.E.*

(*After* BUDDY'S *number two* CROOKS *enter and lurk L.1.E.*)

(*Enter* MOTTY *through door L.C.*)

SWITCHBOARD CUE No. 23.

LEFTY: (*Offering book and pen to* MOTTY) Can I have your autograph, Mister ?

MOTTY: (*Signing*) Why, sure, I'm no Humphrey Bogart.

LEFTY: O.K., Humph, stick 'em up. (MOTTY *raises his hands*).

> TOUCH *sticks a gun in* MOTTY'S *back, while* LEFTY *frisks him, taking articles from pockets and handing them to* TOUCH, *who pouches them.*

LEFTY: Wallet—

MOTTY: Hey, be careful, that's got money in.

LEFTY: That's good news!! (*Producing old-fashioned turnip watch*)—and a flying saucer.

MOTTY: That's my watch.

LEFTY: *Was* your watch.

> PERCY'S *voice is heard off, as he enters cheerfully through door L.C.*

PERCY: Goodnight, fireman. Don't forget, if there's a fire, we're not insured.

LEFTY: (*Sharply to* MOTTY) Put your hands down and keep your mouth shut. (MOTTY *obeys*).

> PERCY *enters and sees* MOTTY.

PERCY: Motty! (*Counting bills*) You went without your money. Five hundred dollars for your hotel bill—Five hundred for Sally's—and a hundred for tips.

> MOTTY, *trembling, takes each wad and puts it in his downstage pocket.*
> TOUCH *transfers each to his downstage pocket.*

PERCY: Come on, aren't you going to introduce me to your pals ?

MOTTY: I-I-I (TOUCH *prods him with gun*) Oooo!

LEFTY: (*Crisply*) Stick 'em up!

PERCY: (*Puzzled*) Stick 'em up ?

LEFTY: (*Louder*) Stick 'em up!

PERCY: Stick what up ?

LEFTY: Put your hands up!

PERCY: Like him ?

LEFTY:	Yeh—like him! (PERCY *puts his hands up*).
MOTTY:	(*Fearfully*) Percy, they're robbers.
	TOUCH *sticks revolver into* MOTTY'S *back.*
	MOTTY *raises his hands.*
MOTTY:	They're after your money. They've taken all mine.
PERCY:	(*Incredulous*) What, all of it? Come on—it's my turn now.
LEFTY:	(*Sourly*) We haven't finished with him yet.
PERCY:	(*Indignantly*) Don't you bother about him! I'm his boss. Come on, mister, I'm the one with all the money.
LEFTY:	Are you. Then you're the one we're waiting for.
PERCY:	Go on. Who recommended you to me?
LEFTY:	(*Nastily*) Wise guy, eh? (*He pats over* PERCY'S *pockets showing fat roll*) Sa-a-y! Touch, look at that! Thanks a lot, mister. (*Shows signs of going*).
PERCY:	(*Alarmed*) Hey, wait a bit! Are you two lads out here every night?
LEFTY:	Well, what of it?
PERCY:	Meet me out here tomorrow night, and I'll have a lot more money on me than that.
MOTTY:	Don't take any notice of him, he's crazy.
LEFTY:	(*In full agreement*) You're telling me. (*Moving over to R. centre*) They'll have come for you from the nut-house by then. Come on, Touch!
	(*They both exit R.1.E.*)
PERCY:	Don't forget, same place, same time and I'll have bundles more money. (*Shouting after them*) After that we'll make it every Tuesday and Thursday at 7.30.
MOTTY:	Percy, say you're drunk!
PERCY:	Drunk? I've never been so sober in my life! I've managed to get rid of fifteen thousand dollars.
	As MOTTY *opens his mouth to reply—sounds of Police whistles and a scuffle off stage R. Re-enter two policemen with wads of notes which were taken from* PERCY.
COP 1:	Here's your dough, Mr. Piggott, and thanks a lot for holding them. Don't worry, Mister, *you'll* get the reward!
PERCY:	(*In horror*) The reward? What reward?
COP 1:	Two thousand dollars, Mr. Piggott—for helping in the arrest! Goodnight.
	Exit Cops R.
PERCY:	(*Miserably*) I've got my money back and two thousand more. Well, what do you know about that?
MOTTY:	(*Looking at him strangely*) I'll tell you what I know, Percy Piggott. That crook was quite right. They *will*

be coming for you from the nuthouse soon!
(*Backs away, looks at him nervously, then bolts and exits L.1.E.*)

>PERCY *shrugs miserably and sinks on crate beside door.*

PERCY: Money!—Money! I can't get rid of the damned stuff.
>ENTER *from door L.C.* SALLY *in trim office suit, carrying a handbag.*

SALLY: Hullo, Percy.

PERCY: (*Joyfully*) Hello, Sally.

SALLY: It's lovely to find you all alone. (*She sits on case C.*)

PERCY: It's lovely to find you all alone, too.

SALLY: I don't see much of you these days.

PERCY: I've been so busy.

SALLY: Busy? Do you call throwing your money around, being " busy " ?

PERCY: Busy's too good a name for it. It's damned hard labour?

SALLY: Then why are you *doing* it ?

PERCY: I wish I could tell you... Sally.

SALLY: Oh, Percy, you're not the careful lad I used to know in Newton-Le-Willows ... the one who used to make such a fuss over two one-and-threes at the pictures.

PERCY: Aye! Do you remember when we used to sit in stalls sucking humbugs ? Sally—let's sneak off to the pictures *now*! (*They both rise from crate and move R.*)

SALLY: Oh yes—no—not with you, Percy—you'd only try and buy the cinema! Besides, haven't you got a date with Miss Lilac Lamore ? (PERCY *sits on R. of crate*).

PERCY: (*Amazed*) Date ? With Lilac ?

SALLY: Aye!

PERCY: But I don't have dates with Lilac. I only *buy* her things!

SALLY: You mean you're not in love with her ?

PERCY: Me in love with Lilac ? Don't be so daft!

SALLY: Oh, Percy!

PERCY: And anyone who says I am is telling lies.

SALLY: (*Sitting on L. of crate*) What's happened ? All of a sudden you're our Percy again. Just as we were back in Newton-Le-Willows, walking home alongside the slag heap.

PERCY: Aye, didn't the gas works smell lovely!!

SALLY: Oh, look (*Looking out and up L. of audience*) there's the same moon.

PERCY: So it is! I thought I recognised it. Fancy them having the same moon over here. It must have followed us, I wonder if it's for sale.

CALL: DANCERS, SINGERS, MOTTY,
CHAUFFEUR, PILOT, SALLY.

MUSIC CUE No. 10: "I OWE YOU"

(SALLY and PERCY)

1 *Verse*, 1 *Refrain*.

SALLY: (*Spoken*) Oh, Percy do stop worrying about money.

VERSE

PERCY: Sally, I'm the worrying kind,
And I must confess
Something that's been on my mind
Always more or less.
Love's a Fifty-fifty game
And I can't forget,
But I find that all the same
You've landed me in debt.

REFRAIN

PERCY: I owe you for being so endearing
When you might have been Heaven knows who.
I owe you, I do, I do, I do, I do.

SALLY: I owe you for all we've done together,
For Moonlight and Evening for two.
I owe you, I do, I do, I do, I do.

PERCY: I'm going to write a business letter,
And say the things that must be said.
A note from your devoted debtor.
And I'll sign at the foot, ' Simply Yours in the Red.'
Sally if I'm blue
It's just because I owe you,
For being too good to be true

SALLY: }
PERCY: } I owe you, I do, I really truly do, I do—I do!

After number MUSIC continues under scene.
PERCY *and* SALLY *are now holding hands.*

PERCY: Oh, Sally, isn't it lovely to be in love!

SALLY: (*Breathlessly*) In love!

PERCY: Well, what do you think I'm doing? Holding your pulse?

SALLY: Percy, you realise what you're saying?

PERCY: No courting, yes I do! (*In alarm, recollecting himself*) (*Rising and moving stage R.C.*) I'd forgotten. Thank you for reminding me, Sally! ... I take it all back!

SALLY: (*Outraged*) (*Rising*) Take it back? *Take it back*? And is that all you've got to say to me, Percy Piggott?

PERCY: You don't understand, Sally. It's just that I've got to *wait.*

SALLY: Wait? Wait for what? As far as I'm concerned you can wait for *ever*!

Act 1 : Sc. 5.   THE PIGGOTT OFFICES, ROCKEFELLER CENTER. Lift is back C. with sliding doors.   French windows and both office doors R. and L.   All practical.

Act 1 : Sc. 5.   Percy Piggott selects a monster cigar and prepares to dictate to his secretaries.

PERCY:	No, Sally—
SALLY:	(*Unable to stop*) You carry on, Mr. Rich Guy. Enjoy yourself! Spend your money on your fur coats and garter girls. You and your Society friends! Friends? Twisters more like. Paula Van Norden and her precious father. They'll soon have your money off you, every penny of it!
PERCY:	(*Hopefully*) Do you really think so?
SALLY:	Then see how much time they've got for Percy Piggott from Newton-Le-Willows *when he's broke*. Do you hear me, broke—broke— (*Makes a hasty, tearful exit L.*)
PERCY:	Oh, Sally, Sally—oh, women—women—why can't they understand! They never do know what they want—until they get it—and when they do—they don't want it!!
PERCY:	Money, money! I'm sick of the damned stuff! (*He tears up two or three dollar bills and surreptitiously drops them behind packing case R. of stage door.*)
PERCY:	Oh, Sally! All right—I'll show you! From now on, I'm going to spend myself daft.

TABS close on start of reprise.

MUSIC CUE No. 11 REPRISE:

"SAVING UP FOR SALLY"
(PERCY)

PERCY:	I'm spending all for Sally

      Spending for a rainy day
At first I could have laughed
      It all seemed kind of daft
But now—by gum, I've got the trick
      I'm getting rid of money quick
I'm not a lad to dally
      Of Sally I'm as proud as I can be,
This is where I really do begin
      I'm straining every nerve to win
The love that Sally's saving up for me!

(PERCY *exit R.1.E.*)

SWITCHBOARD CUE No. 24.

BLACK OUT

ACT 1
SCENE 5 (Playing Time: 30 mins.)
SWITCHBOARD CUE No. 25.

MUSIC CUE No. 11A SEGUE FROM REPRISE OF SALLY TO

MUSIC CUE No. 12 OFFICE BALLET.

THE PIGGOTT OFFICES, ROCKEFELLER CENTER. MORNING.

CALL: BUDDY, PERCY, POLICEMEN.

Characters in this scene:
MOTTY
STENOGRAPHER 1
CHAUFFEUR
PILOT
BUDDY
SALLY
POLICEMEN
PERCY
STENOGRAPHER 2
BOY
STENOGRAPHER 3
PAULA
VAN NORDEN
SINGERS AND DANCERS

A ridiculously luxurious modern office on an upper floor of a skyscraper. By no stretch of imagination could it be too eccentric. Upstage are the private elevator I.C. and open windows L. with a magnificent view of the mid-town skyline. R. is an archway leading to the reception lobby, down L. a door labelled MISS WHITTLE, R. a door labelled MR. WHITTLE. R. Furniture includes a magnificent desk with telephone L., a ticker tape machine, various magnificent chairs, 1 desk R. and a couch directly in front of it.
WHEN THE CURTAIN OPENS the STAFF is doing the Office Ballet.

No. 12 OFFICE BALLET

At end of Ballet ENTER MOTTY *L.1.E. He looks round in disgust.*

MOTTY: And what's going on here? Is this office going crazy? (*The office staff exit L. and R. Lift Boy goes into lift. The stenographers only remain on stage*). (*To seven stenographers*) What are you girls doing?

STENOG. 1: Nothing, Mr. Whittle. We're Mr. Piggott's personal stenographers.

MOTTY: What, all seven of you?

STENOG. 1: Why yes. Mr. Piggott has seven copies of every letter!

MOTTY: Has he never heard of carbon paper?

STENOG. 1: Why, no. Mr. Piggott says carbon copies look *cheap*! (*Stenographers exit through door R.*)

MOTTY: (*Raising his hands*) Carbon copies cheap!

ENTER CHAUFFEUR *from R.U. arch.*

CHAUFFEUR: Oh, Boss!

MOTTY:	(*To Chauffeur*) And what do *you* want?
CHAUFFEUR:	Excuse me, Sir, I wants to know, Boss, which of the automobiles Mr. Piggott wants this afternoon, the Rolls? The Bentley? The Packard? The Jaguar or the Hispano Suiza!
MOTTY:	Mr. Piggott can take a taxi!
CHAUFFEUR:	Yes, sir. We bought a couple of taxi-cabs last week.

> MOTTY *does a "take" as EXIT* CHAUFFEUR *through Arch.*
>
> *ENTER from Window L. man in* PILOT'S *clothes.*

PILOT:	Hey, bud, are you called Mr. Whittle?
MOTTY:	(*Dazed*) No—aye, I think so . . .
PILOT:	I just delivered the helicopter.
MOTTY:	(*Gasping*) Helicopter!
PILOT:	It's upstairs on the roof.
MOTTY:	(*After a quick look through window*) But what do we want a helicopter for?
PILOT:	Mr. Piggott said to get up to his apartment.
MOTTY:	Get up to his apartment? But dammit, we've got six lifts.
PILOT:	Sure, but he says " How's he to get home if there's an elevator strike? "

> *EXIT through window L.*

MOTTY:	Oh, he did, did he?

> *ENTER* SALLY *from L.1.E. with batch of cheques and pen tray, which she puts on desk.*

SALLY:	What's the matter, Daddy?
MOTTY:	Helicopters—that's what's the matter.
SALLY:	(*Laying cheques on desk*) We certainly are getting busy these days!
MOTTY:	Busy?—In *this* office? (*Sarcastically*) It's a hive of industry—filled with the idlest lot of bees . . .
SALLY:	I'm working double overtime—just writing out cheques for Percy to sign!

> *THREE* GIRLS *walk from L.1.E. to R.2.E. with arms in slings.*

MOTTY:	(*Sarcastically*) Is this *all*? (*Looking at girls as they pass him*). What's wrong with them?
SALLY:	Writer's cramp, we've had to break.
MOTTY:	(*Looking through cheques*) Ten thousand dollars? Seventeen thousand dollars? Twenty-five thousand dollars? (*Startled*) Sixty thousand dollars? What's *this*?
SALLY:	For a place called the Willowbank Racing Stable!

MOTTY: A racing stable. What's he want with a racing stable?
     (SALLY *walks over R. to couch and almost*
     bursts in tears).

SALLY: Perhaps he needs it to keep the helicopter in!

MOTTY: Eh, what's the matter, love, you feeling poorly?
     (*Walking over to couch and sitting on left arm*).

SALLY: Nonsense, Dad, its' nothing really—
     MUSIC CUE No. 13:
      "TROUBLE WITH MY HEART"

MOTTY: You can't fool your old dad—I know when summat's
     wrong.
     SWITCHBOARD CUE No. 26.

     No. 13: "TROUBLE WITH MY HEART"
       (MOTTY and SALLY)
      1 *Verse*, 1 *Refrain, 2nd Refrain*
        VERSE 1.

MOTTY: I saw you through the measles,
(*Spoken to* The whooping cough and mumps!
tempo of I poulticed you in Morecambe
Music)   When you came out in lumps
     I coped with scarlet fever
      And chicken pox, by gum.
     I'm family physician,
      So let diseases come.

SALLY: Though you're very darling, very dear
      I've got to deal with this myself, I fear ...
       REFRAIN
     Trouble with my heart!
      That's what's wrong with me
     I've got every single symptom that there can be.
     Trembling like a leaf,
     Tearful and distrait
      I get more of a problem ev'ry day!
     On my fever chart
      (SALLY *rises and walks over L. and sits on desk*)
     There's an upward curve
     Where he smiled at someone else—and I lost my nerve!
     Maybe I'm a fool.
     Maybe I'm not smart,
      But I know that I'm sure of the cure for my
       troublesome heart!

MOTTY: (*Rising from couch and walking to stage C.*)
(*Spoken*) I know how it is, love; I was just the same at your age.
     Do you know when I was courting your mother, she,
     bless her dear heart, seemed to fancy the ginger-headed
     chap who had the milk round. I got such a pain it was
     worse than appendicitis and painters' colic rolled into
     one.

SALLY: *(Spoken)* *(Sung)*:	Poor old Dad, I guess we Whittles never ought to do anything so silly as falling in love.

SALLY: *(Spoken)* *(Sung)*: On my fever chart
    There's an upward curve
Where he smiled at someone else—and I lost my nerve!
    Maybe I'm a fool.
Maybe I'm not smart,
    But I know that I'm sure of the cure for my
    troublesome heart!

SWITCHBOARD CUE No. 27.

ENTER BUDDY, *through Arch. R. carrying a newspaper.*

MOTTY: It was a black day when Percy paled up with those Van Nordens!

SALLY: *(Indignantly)* They're ruining him!

MOTTY: What does he think it's going to get him ? That's what beats me!

BUDDY: Maybe that's the answer. *(Showing newspaper)*.

MOTTY: Where ? *(Taking newspaper from* BUDDY*)*.

BUDDY: *(Pointing)* There. Ellenberg's Gossip column!

SALLY: *(Looking)* About Percy!

BUDDY: *(Taking newspaper from* MOTTY*)* About Percy ? Get a load of this! *(Reads)* " All Manhattan is asking why Percy Piggott, millionaire dimwit, not content with financing ' Garter Girl,' the likeliest looking flop show of the Season, is throwing his money around town like a cock-eyed mariner. Does Big Boy from Newton-Le-Willows reckon heavy spending will dazzle the beautiful Paula Van Norden and secure him a classy bride!"

MOTTY: *(Indignantly)* That's libel. *That's* what that is.

SALLY: I don't suppose Percy'll mind.

BUDDY: *(Angrily)* To heck with Percy! I don't like it. He can't treat Lilac Delany like that! *(Moving up stage C.)*

MOTTY: Damn Lilac Delany! What about my Sally?

SALLY: Don't worry about me, Dad. Percy can do what he likes.

MOTTY: *(Boiling)* Oh, can he ? How many *more* women does he want—the blasted mormon!

BUDDY: Let me get my hands on him, that's all. *(Moving down Stage C.)*

Telephone rings.

BUDDY: *(Grabs phone)* Hello, who is this ? ... What ? Are you kidding ? *(With growing anxiety)* You don't mean it ? ... What, any time ? ... Thanks for the tip off! *(Solemnly replacing receiver)*. Holy mike!

OTHERS: What is it ?

BUDDY: The Van N   ⁻ɔnk ...

OTHERS:	Well, go on!
BUDDY:	They're in trouble . . . bad trouble. They may have to close down!
MOTTY:	But Percy's got two hundred and fifty thousand dollars in that bank.
BUDDY:	That much?
MOTTY:	Well, what are we going to *do*?
SALLY:	Do—do— (*Stamping her foot*). Don't stand there twittering!
MOTTY:	(*Aggrieved*) Twittering? Who's twittering?
SALLY:	Dad—you get Percy on the phone. Tell him to come over here right away. Hurry. (MOTTY *starts phoning*). I'll make out a cheque for the money and we'll draw it out before the bank closes! We must save him, whatever happens. Tell a messenger to stand by.
BUDDY:	Attagirl!

EXIT R.2.E.

MOTTY:	(*To telephone*) Hello? Mr. Piggott's apartment? I want Mr. Piggott. Not there? . . . What? He what? (*Replaces receiver*) Well, that's torn it.
SALLY:	What's the matter?
MOTTY:	Percy went out an hour ago . . . with a pair of scissors.
SALLY:	Went out? (*Puzzled*) With a pair of scissors?
MOTTY:	Aye, perhaps he's going to cut himself off with a shilling!

RE-ENTER BUDDY *R.2.E. Bell rings. Lights flash on elevator.* STAFF *begin to hurry on.*

BUDDY:	Here he comes now.
SALLY:	Just in time. I'll make out the cheque. Buddy, will you come with me to cash it?

EXIT L.1.E.

BUDDY:	Sure, I'll go and cash it.

EXIT L.1.E.

MUSIC CUE No. 13A. *Lift Music.*

(MOTTY *sits on chair R. of desk*)

P.A.S.:	Attention please! Attention please! Calling all floors . . . Mr. Piggott is just disembarking from his Cadillac . . . He's entering the Piggott Building! . . . He's safely in the elevator! . . . He's rising to the fiftieth floor at the rate of seventy floors per half-minute . . . He's made it!

Chord in orchestra as lift door opens.

STAFF *line up as elevator stops. Door opens disclosing* PERCY *carrying an armful of chrysanthemums. In attendance on him are two cops.*

PERCY: Good morning all!

STAFF: Good morning, Mr. Piggott!

PERCY: Nice weather we're having!

STAFF: Yes, Mr. Piggott!

PERCY: Lots of nice weather to come.

STAFF: Is there?

PERCY: All next week's not touched yet!

MOTTY: (*Truculently*) And where have you been, may I ask?

PERCY: Picking flowers.

MOTTY: Picking flowers? And why the bodyguard? (*Rising*).

COP 1: He was picking them in Central Park!

MOTTY: But you can get fined for that!

COP 2: He was. The judge sent us along to collect the money. (*Handing slip*).

PERCY: (*Happily*) Five hundred dollars. Pay up, Motty, and look pleasant.

COP 1: Five hundred.

MOTTY *wearily takes out a large wad and pays.*

PERCY: Go on, don't be stingy. Give 'em fifty dollars each for a drink.

MOTTY *with a look of suffering does so.*

COP 2: Why, thanks a lot, Mr. Piggott.

COP 1: Any time you want any more flowers, don't forget Central Park.

EXEUNT COPS *into lift.*

PERCY: (*Tenderly*) They are all for *you*, Motty. (*Hands him flowers*) And I'll take the petty cash! (*Takes money from* MOTTY).

MOTTY: *Petty cash!* Five hundred dollars for chysanthemomiums.

PERCY: They're not chrysanthemomiums—they're Rosidandriums!

MOTTY *exits with flowers L.1.E. in exasperation.*

Everybody happy?

STENOGS.: Oh yes, Mr. Piggott!

GIRL 1: (*Enters from Arch R.2.E. with gold cigar box and hands* PERCY *a cigar, saying*) Your cigar, Mr. Piggott. (*She exits L.1.E. with cigar box*).

GIRL 2:	Your matches, Mr. Piggott (*and exits L.1.E.* PERCY *lights cigar—struggling to draw through it*).
PERCY:	By gum—I'll draw the shirt off my back doing this! (*He coughs*) It's like smoking Clarke's Blood Mixture! —I'd rather be at home with a woodbine!
PERCY:	(*Sitting at desk*) Now let's get down to business. (*Studies letters*) Here's an interesting little proposition, ladies. Take down! (*The girls look at him*). Take down seven letters.
GIRLS:	(*Raising books*) Yes, Mr. Piggott!
PERCY:	No, no, make it seven telegrams, they're dearer. (*Dictates*) " To Oscar Faraday, Esq., 10, East 63rd Street, New York City. 'Phone Butterfield, 8. Stroke 9067. Dear Sir, In answer to your letter asking if I will finance your latest invention I shall be delighted to do so, and am accordingly wiring you herewith the sum of five thousand dollars in advance. Go right ahead, big boy. Stop." No that doesn't sound right. " Go right ahead, big boy, and don't stop. Stop. Build a factory, if necessary build two factories. Spare no expense. The market is wide open for your product. Yours sincerely, Percy Piggott."
	GIRLS *lower their books.*
PERCY:	Oh and " P.S." (*Girls have raised their books again*). Kindly say in your next letter what it is you have invented!" That'll be all ladies, thank you.
GIRLS:	Thank you, Mr. Piggott.
	EXEUNT R.2.E.
	ENTER SALLY, BUDDY *and* MOTTY (*L.1.E.*) *with cheque.*
SALLY:	Percy, will you please sign this right away ?
PERCY:	(*Studying cheque*) Two hundred thousand dollars. That's grand. (*Pleased*) Now how did I manage to spend *all that* ?
MOTTY:	You haven't spent it, we're going to *save* it for you.
PERCY:	(*Alarmed*) Save it ?
MOTTY:	Your Park Avenue gent, Mr. Van Norden. His bank is going bust and we're taking your money out! (*Moving to R.C.*)
SALLY:	Sign it, Percy. Do hurry, please. It may be too late!
PERCY:	(*Rising*) Then let it be too late. I want it to be too late. I'm not taking any of my money out of that bank! (*Moving to C.*)
OTHERS:	*Wha—at!*
SALLY:	You're not ?

PERCY:	It wouldn't be sporting! Now listen, Motty—supposing you had a bank that was getting a bit dicky. Would *you* want your friends taking their money out ?
BUDDY:	Mr. Piggott, please think again. (*Moving to Percy's L.*)
ALL:	Please.
PERCY:	I have thunk again. (*Deliberately tearing cheque in half*). I'll leave money where it is!
BUDDY:	Holy mike!
PERCY:	You understand, don't you, Sally ?
SALLY:	(*Strung up*) Yes, I understand—perfectly. Your fine *friends* come first!

EXIT L.1.E.

PERCY:	Sally! Sally, come back! Here boy. (BOY *enters from Arch. R.*). (*Gives dollar bills*) Run out and buy Miss Whittle some roses.
BOY:	Sure, Mr. Piggott, how many ?
PERCY:	Oh, about an office full. Oh, and Boy, take a taxi.
BOY:	Yes, sir!
PERCY:	And, Boy, (*Peeling off another note*) take two taxis.
BOY:	Yes, sir!
PERCY:	Boy—take three taxis—and run in between them.

ENTER GIRL with tea from R.2.E.

BOY:	Yes, sir. (*He exits quickly through Arch R.* PERCY *sits at desk R.*)
GIRL:	Your tea, Mr. Piggott. (*She puts tray on table and exits L.1.E.*)
PERCY:	What's the matter with Sally, Motty ?
MOTTY:	(*Throwing newspaper on right end of desk*) The matter with Sally is that she can read! ! (*He moves behind desk to* PERCY'S *L.*)
PERCY:	Oh, heck, has she seen that ?
BUDDY:	You bet. And (*Threateningly*) *I've* seen it, too!
MOTTY:	Well, what are you going to do about it ? (*Moving down to L. of* PERCY).
PERCY:	I'm not going to do anything. (*Pouring tea from pot into cup*) (*Pause*) I've *done* it!
BUDDY:	You mean you've seen Ellenberg ? What happened ? (*Moving to R. of desk*).
PERCY:	You go over to the hospital and take a look! (*Putting milk into tea cup*).
BUDDY:	You socked him ?
PERCY:	No, I just gave him a tuppenny one!
MOTTY:	But he'll sue you for that! ! !

D

PERCY:	I hope so. As I drove him to the hospital, he mumbled something about ten thousand dollars. But I settled out of court.
BUDDY:	Smart work!
PERCY:	Aye . . . I gave him fifteen thousand. (*Pouring tea from cup into saucer and drinking*).
MOTTY:	Fifteen thousand! Percy Piggott, have you any idea of your present financial position ? (*Looking into tea cup as though reading his fortune*).
PERCY:	Wild, wet and windy!!
MOTTY:	Picking flowers! Clouting columnists! (*Moving below desk to* PERCY'S *R.*) And what about the racing stable ?
PERCY:	Oh, that. I bought it for my horse!
MOTTY:	And where did you get a horse ?
PERCY:	In a night club.
BUDDY:	A horse in a night club ?
PERCY:	Not horse—chap who owned it. Its running in the big race this afternoon. I've got five thousand dollars on it to win!
BUDDY:	Gee, that's a lot of money.
MOTTY:	What's the horse called ?
PERCY:	Good manners.
BUDDY:	(*In despair*) Oh, no, not *that*! (*Collapses on couch R.*)
MOTTY:	What's wrong with it ?
BUDDY:	Everything, except its name. It manners are so good that when the tapes go up it says to the other horses " After you." (PERCY *does a lot of miming of the tape going up—and the horse " Good Manners" motioning the other horses to go first*).
MOTTY:	And youve put five thousand dollars on it!
BUDDY:	Let me lay it off for you, Mr. Piggott. (*Rising from couch*).

ENTER STENOGRAPHER 3 *L.1.E.*

STENOG. 3:	Oh, Mr. Piggott.
PERCY:	What is it, love ?
STENOG. 3:	You asked me to remind you about that stock you bought . . . United Fertilizer.
PERCY:	Thank you, love. (*Takes out money*) Buy yourself a box of chocolates.
STENOG. 3:	Thank you, sir. (*She exits L.1.E.*)
MOTTY:	Percy, you've not bought United Fertilizer ?
PERCY:	Why shouldn't I ?
MOTTY:	There's been a bumper harvest. Nobody's buying fertilizers now. There'll be a slump!
PERCY:	Are you sure—can I depend on that ?

BUDDY:	Yes, Mr. Piggott. You call your broker right away.
PERCY:	Thanks for the suggestion. (*Picking up phone*) Ask them to get me Mr. Alison on the phone quick.
MOTTY:	That's better, Percy. You've got to pull up somewhere. Your bank balance just won't stand it.

Phone rings.

PERCY:	(*Taking up phone*) Hello. Hello ? Is that Mr. Alison ? Percy Piggott here. How are you ? How's the wife ? What another ? That's *three* Golf Trophies she's got now! Mr. Alison, I want you to buy me another ten thousand shares in United Fertilizer.

MOTTY *and* BUDDY *register despair.*

PERCY:	Aye, that's okay. Send over right away and Mr. Whittle'll give you a cheque.

CALL: PAULA.

MOTTY:	Mr. Whittle won't.
PERCY:	Mr. Whittle will. Yes—I know everyone says it's a bad time to buy but I've got a reason. Oh, and Mr. Alison, do you happen to have a bookmaker ? You have ? Then be a pal and put two thousand to win on " Good Manners," for the Big Race this afternoon. Yes, thanks—thanks a lot. Cheeri-bye. What ? Oh, no—don't *you* back it ! ! (*Puts down phone*).

The OTHERS *are looking at him as though he was crazy.*

PERCY:	You know you lads don't understand this money business.
MOTTY:	No we don't, do we Percy ?
PERCY:	(*Walking towards settee—*MOTTY *facing him and walking backwards,* BUDDY *following close behind* PERCY). This high finance, Motty, is very complicated.

MOTTY *and* BUDDY *gently lower* PERCY *on the settee.*

MOTTY:	Yes lad—you'd better come and have a sit down!
PERCY:	To make money—you've got to spend it.
BUDDY:	You don't say!
PERCY:	Yes, I'll explain it all to you. Now for argument's sake, we'll take the upward curve of expenditure which we'll call ' Y.'
BUDDY:	Which we'll call ' Y '!
PERCY:	And the downward curve of income which we'll call ' X.'
BUDDY:	Which we'll call ' X.'
PERCY:	Now ' X ' and ' Y ' are going up and down like this! (*Up and down arm movement*) Should they happen to touch in passing—wallop, Mrs. Cox—your mother's won a duck!

BUDDY:	She has ? Well, we certainly live and learn!
PERCY:	Aye, I was chatting it over with a banker!
MOTTY:	(*Unable to stand it*) And I bet his name was James Van Norden? (*Taking out paper*) Here's your balance sheet, Mr. Piggott. Feast your eye on it, lad. In my opinion you ought to see a psychy—iartrist.

EXIT furiously R.1.E.

PERCY:	(*Laughing*) What the hell's he talking about ?
BUDDY:	A psychiatrist!
PERCY:	And what's a psychiatrist when he's at home ?
BUDDY:	(*Soothingly*) He's an expensive kind of doctor who looks after poor tired business men.

BUDDY *looks nervously at* PERCY.

PERCY:	Expensive, eh ?
BUDDY:	Oh, very.
PERCY:	Oh, good—I'll have a couple of them!

BUDDY *utters a moan and bolts for his life R.2.E.* PERCY *rises and goes C.*
ENTER *Boys with armloads of roses.*
Telephone rings, PERCY *answers.*

PERCY:	Oh, Miss Van Norden—send her up, please. (*Seeing boys with flowers*) What's them ?
BOYS:	Flowers for Miss Whittle, sir.
PERCY:	Take 'em in her office, there's good lads.

CALL: VAN NORDEN.

BOYS:	Okay, sir.

EXEUNT Boys L.2.E. PERCY *sits at desk and studies balance sheet carefully, chuckling with satisfaction.*
LIFT *is seen coming up.*
Lift door opens and ENTER PAULA, gorgeously dressed as usual.

BOY:	Miss Van Norden.
PERCY:	Hello, Paula my dear. Come in and sit down. Have you had your tea, what a pity, I've just had mine. (PAULA *sits on R. of couch,* PERCY *L. of couch*).
PAULA:	So this is where you work ?
PERCY:	Do you like it ?
PAULA:	Rather overwhelming, isn't it—for an office ? You've never told me exactly what your business *is*!
PERCY:	Well, call it Frenzied Finance.
PAULA:	(*Amused*) Frenzied Finance? And how are you doing?
PERCY:	I can't grumble, I'm spending money.
PAULA:	Yes, you are, aren't you, Percy.

PERCY:	And you don't know it, but you've been a great help.
PAULA:	(*Softly*) Have I ? (*After pause*) Percy, did you happen to see Ellenberg's Column this afternoon ?
PERCY:	Aye. And I saw Ellenberg, too!
PAULA:	Of course he had no right to make such a fabulous statement.
PERCY:	I hope it didn't annoy you, Paula.
PAULA:	The idea of our being engaged ? Well, I admit it was a little surprising. After all, we've only known each other for a little while ... though we do have fun, don't we ?
PERCY:	Oh, is that what they call it ? It's getting warm isn't it ? (*Nervously changing the subject*).
PAULA:	Oh, Percy, are you always as shy as this ? Have you never done any courting ?
PERCY:	Well, only once—to oblige a pal of mine who had 'flu— and couldn't go!!
PAULA:	Have you ever put your arm around a girl's waist ? (*Moving closely to* PERCY).
PERCY:	Aye, I've done that!
PAULA:	And taken her down a country lane ? And you kissed her ?
PERCY:	Aye, I've done that!
PAULA:	And when you've come to a stile—and the moon is shining—you've—
PERCY:	Aye, I've done that!! How's your father ?
PAULA:	Very worried, poor man. That's really why I came to see you. There's a run on the bank and I'm afraid Father may lose everything.
PERCY:	You tell him not to worry, I'm leaving my money where it is.
PAULA:	Oh, Percy! (*Cuddling up to* PERCY).
PERCY:	Have you enough room ?
PAULA:	You'll risk the bank going smash ? I think you're the most wonderful man in the world! (PAULA *strokes his face caressingly—and* PERCY *gradually passes out*).
PERCY:	Oh, Mother, your lad's slipping! I'd do anything for your Father.
PAULA:	You can pretend that it's all for Father—but I know better.
PERCY:	You don't know the half of it!
PAULA:	Oh yes, I do.
PERCY:	Oh no, you don't.
PAULA:	A girl has instincts you know.
PERCY:	Do you have them an' all? You ought to try bicarbonate of soda!

PAULA: (*Close to him*) That newspaper story...may have embarrassed *you* for *my* sake but I guess I just don't care!

By this time she has PERCY *leaning backwards over the desk.*

(*Lusciously*) Percy! (*attempting to kiss him*).

PERCY: Mother, Mother! Help! Help somebody, come!

ENTER SALLY *from L.2.E. who sees situation.*

Look out, Sally! (*They both rise from couch*).

SALLY: I hate to interrupt a business conference, Mr. Piggott, but I thought you'd like to know that Mr. Van Norden is on his way up!

EXIT L.2.E.

PAULA: Father here? I wonder what that can mean...

Elevator door opens, releasing JAMES VAN NORDEN, *who walks down centre.*

—Father, great news—Percy's standing by the bank.

VAN NORDEN: My boy, I can't thank you enough, but your gallant action has come too late.

PAULA: Father!

VAN NORDEN: Another half-hour and we'd have been all right but the City Fire Department have called up to say that they're sending over a cheque for three hundred thousand dollars and want the cash right away. (*Sitting on chair R. of desk*).

PAULA: The cash? Father!

VAN NORDEN: Forgive an old man for taking this so badly, Piggott, but the Van Norden Bank has been my pride and joy, my baby. I've nursed it through good times and bad and somehow I just can't face up to the fact that in a few moments its door will be closed for ever. (*During this speech* PERCY *gradually begins to cry—and at the end— he is wiping his eyes with his handkerchief*).

PERCY: Don't worry. We'll keep 'em open!

VAN NORDEN: Piggott, you don't mean...you can't mean!!! (*Rising and moving down R.C. to* PERCY).

PERCY: You can have that three hundred thousand dollars in cash right away—and with pleasure. (PERCY *moves upstage to behind desk L.C.,* VAN NORDEN *moves over to stage R.C.*).

VAN NORDEN: But suppose the worst happens. Suppose there's a run from another direction before closing time.

PERCY: Then we'll have had a try, won't we? Motty! Sally! Buddy! Come quick—

PERCY *sits at desk and whips out cheque book. ENTER* MOTTY *R.1.E.,* BUDDY *R.2.E., and* SALLY *L.1.E,*

Motty, how much money have we got in the Manhattan Trust Bank downstairs ?

MOTTY : About three hundred thousand dollars. Why ? (MOTTY *moves to C.*)

PERCY : Three hundred thousand ? Lovely! (*Scribbles cheque*). Take this cheque. Get downstairs quick and bring it back in cash!—All of it—in cash—remember—in cash! Right away.

MOTTY : (*With a suspicious look at* VAN NORDEN) What for ?

PERCY : For Mr. Van Norden. I'm not seeing his bank go smash for the sake of a paltry three hundred thousand dollars.

MOTTY : I refuse! (*Turning and walking up stage*).

PERCY : Sally!

SALLY : So do I.

PERCY : Then you go, Buddy. (*Hands him the cheque*). Hurry! Don't argue—go downstairs and bring it up in cash right away. Do you hear ? In cash!!

> BUDDY *makes an appealing gesture to* MOTTY *and bolts for his life, R.2.E.*

VAN NORDEN : I must get back to my bank. It's going to be touch and go. Come, Paula. Bless you, Piggott.

> *EXIT through arch R.*

PAULA : And that goes for me, too, Percy dear. I know and understand. (*Kisses him lightly and EXITS through arch R.*)

PERCY : (*Looking at* SALLY) Just getting a bit of muck out of my eye! (*Mopping his brow, sitting on settee*) By gum, what a lucky break!

MOTTY : Then I'll give you another lucky break. Percy Piggott, you can accept my resignation.

PERCY : Now, Motty—

MOTTY : Don't you " Now, Motty " me. I'm fed up and finished and far from home! (*He exits R. through office door*).

PERCY : Go and talk to him, Sally, make him see sense.

SALLY : I can't make him see what isn't there. (*Turning away from him*).

PERCY : You're angry with me about Paula.

SALLY : Not at all. I hope you'll both be very happy . . .

PERCY : You ought to thank her, you know.

SALLY : I'm beginning to think so.

PERCY : You don't know what she's doing for us.

SALLY : (*Incredulous*) Doing for *us* ? (*Turning to him*).

PERCY : Aye, she's our best pal if you only knew it!

SALLY : (*Solemnly*) Now I know what they are saying about you is true! The money's gone to your head. You don't know what you're doing.

PERCY:	So you think I'm daft, too ? I know I look a bit peculiar at times but there's nothing wrong with me, Sally—nothing—I only want time—and if you'll give me just a little longer, I can prove it to you!
P.A.S.:	Attention, please—attention, please. Calling Mr. Piggott! Calling Mr. Piggott! Your money is on the way up.
PERCY:	Now we're getting somewhere. Just hold on, Sally, and you'll see!

ENTER BUDDY *R.2.E....*

BUDDY:	Okay, Mr. Piggott, I made it!
PERCY:	Good lad, I'll take it down to the Van Norden Bank myself.
BUDDY:	Yourself ? Who do you think you are—Tarzan ? Come on in, boys.

> *FROM LIFT ENTER* 2 ARMED GUARDS *with guns and* 8 *sacks of money carried by office boys.* STAFF *begin to gather excitedly. Boys drop money bags C.*

PERCY:	What the blood and sands is all *this* ? (*Looking at bags C. stage*).
BUDDY:	Your three hundred thousand dollars in cash. The bank hadn't enough big bills, so we had to take what we could.

ENTER MOTTY *excitedly R.1.E.*

MOTTY:	Percy! Percy!
PERCY:	Go away, Motty. You've sacked yourself.
MOTTY:	I take it back, I take it back—every word of it. I'm proud of you. Why, lad, you're a financial genius ...

> *General excited interest.*

	Haven't you seen the ticker tape ?
PERCY:	What are you blithering about, Motty. What's happened ? (*Moving to* MOTTY *R.C.*)
MOTTY:	(*Triumphantly*) *United Fertilizer*!

> BUDDY *and* SALLY *dash to the ticker.*

PERCY:	Go on! What *about* it ?
MOTTY:	The United States Government, Percy ...
PERCY:	What about the United States Government ?
MOTTY:	*They're going to fertilize the Sahara Desert*!
PERCY:	Oh, *no*! (*Sinking on to couch R.*)
MOTTY:	Aye, there's a boom!
BUDDY:	(*At tape*) The stock's jumped fifteen points—it's up to sixty-five already!
MOTTY:	Think of it, Lad! All that sand turning into *millions*!
PERCY:	Millions ? (*With horror*) But it can't. You must stop it!

Act 1 : Sc. 7.   THE SEA SHORE.

'Buddy' features "Running Away To Land."   Act 2 : Sc. 7.

'RARATONGA'
a sequence in the
Island Ballet.
Act 2 : Sc. 6.

'Percy' makes a conquest and
is carried in state to the island
ceremonies.   Act 2 : Sc. 6.

MOTTY:	Nothing can stop you, you clever lad! You and your X's and Y's and wallop Mrs. Cox, your mother's won a duck.
BUDDY:	(*Pulling out tape*) By Jiminy. Fertilizer's over seventy-seven already—and going up!
PERCY:	You let me look! (*Snatches tape from* BUDDY *and wanders round paying it out*). United Fertilizer seventy-nine... United Fertilizer eighty... United Fertilizer eighty-two...
EVERYBODY:	Eighty-two!
PERCY:	(*Dashing to desk*) Give me that telephone, quick! Give me Alison and McCabe, quick!
MOTTY:	That's the lad. Buy anything you can get!
PERCY:	Buy, you fathead! I'm going to *sell*!
ALL:	(*In horror*) *Sell*! It's reaching eighty-five.
MOTTY:	(*In horror*) *Sell*?
PERCY:	Aye, before I'm ruined! (*To phone*) Get me Alison and McCabe quick. (*To* MOTTY) This is all *your* fault. You promised me this stock wasn't any good! (*To phone*) Alison and McCabe—quick!
	ENTER PAULA *and* VAN NORDEN *excitedly R.2.E.*
	They both move down to Stage R.C.
PAULA:	Oh, Percy, have you heard?
PERCY:	Aye, (*grimly*) I've heard all right. There's your dad's loose change. Tell 'em to take it away—and quick! (*To Van Norden*) I'm sorry, Mister, but I'm in a bit of a crisis! Go and have a cup of tea—and a crumpet!
BUDDY:	United has hit ninety-three!
VAN NORDEN:	But my boy, you don't understand. I shan't need this cash.
PERCY:	What, not need it?
PAULA:	No, Percy. Father's bank is saved!
PERCY:	(*Gasping*) *Saved*?
VAN NORDEN:	Yes, sir. And (*proudly*) *your* original deposit is saved with it!
PERCY:	Saved? Then I'm ruined. (*Imploringly*) Oh, Mister, do take the money, please. Something might happen!
VAN NORDEN:	Not on your life, Mr. Piggott. It so happens that the Van Norden Bank was one of the biggest backers of *United Fertilizers*!
PERCY:	Oh, that blasted stuff *again*!
BUDDY:	It's hitting ninety-eight!
MOTTY:	Ninety-eight! Only two more for game.
PERCY:	Give me a line, I'll get them myself. (*Starts dialling*) (*Rattling the phone desperately*).

BUDDY: Mr. Piggott, think what you're doing!

SALLY: Percy, for my sake—*please*! (SALLY *is sitting on down-stage L. of desk*).

PERCY: But, Sally, it's for your sake I'm doing it!

MOTTY: Doing it for her sake! Now I know you're crazy!

PERCY: (*Dropping phone and jumping up wildly*) And wouldn't you be crazy if you had money pouring in on you? (*Looking at sacks*) Money! Money! Money! You can't get rid of the stuff! (*Kicking sacks*).

There is general agitation.

VAN NORDEN: (*Solemnly*) Poor young fellow! It's been too much for him, becoming a multi-millionaire!

MUSIC CUE No. 14: "ZIP GOES A MILLION."

CHORUS *whisper till last eight bars then sing to end.*

PERCY: (*Hoarsely, staring into space*) A multi-millionaire... A multi-millionaire... multi-millionaire...

All watch him sympathetically, especially SALLY. PERCY'S *trance is snapped by the sudden ringing of the phone.*

MUSIC CUE No. 14: ACT FINALE

"ZIP GOES A MILLION" (*REPRISE*)

Music under dialogue.

(*All* CHORUS *start whispering chorus of "Zip Goes A Million."*)

PERCY: —Alison and McCabe at last! (*Grabs phone*) Yes, it's Percy Piggott speaking. What's that? (*Horrified*) Oh, no! No? (*Drops receiver and registers intense despair*) By gum, I'm done for—*finished*! (*Coming downstage C.*)

ALL: Percy, what's happened?

PERCY: What's happened? What's happened? That blasted horse "Good Manners" has *won*—at a hundred to one!!

As PERCY *collapses* (*in amongst money bags, centre*) *all sing.*

QUICK CURTAIN
AND STRAIGHT UP AGAIN

ALL: Sing "ZIP GOES A MILLION, AND A MILLION—PERCY PIGGOTT'S IN TOWN!"

SWITCHBOARD CUE No. 28.

CURTAIN

END OF ACT I.

ACT II

"RARATONGA" (A TROPICAL ISLAND)

CALL: MUSICAL DIRECTOR, MURU, LELANI, SINGERS, DANCERS, SAILORS, SALLY.

Characters in this scene:

LELANI	BUDDY
MURU	SAILOR 1
SALLY	SAILOR 2
PERCY	SINGERS AND DANCERS

The island to which PERCY has brought his friends in the yacht "Pleasure Cruise." A grove of tangled palm trees with a distant vista of the lagoon. A rocky ledge descends in a series of irregular natural "steps" to a pool fringed with tropical vegetation. The time is evening and the scene colourful.

WHEN THE CURTAIN RISES the stage is apparently empty—although actually here and there are the ISLAND GIRLS, their backs to the audience, long dark hair flowing over their shoulders.

SWITCHBOARD CUE No. 30.

MUSIC CUE No. 15. COURTSHIP BALLET.

(*See* DANCE PLOT)

To music with the mounting monotonous excitement of Ravel's *Bolero*, LELANI, a native girl, and MURU, a boy, dance their courtship, beginning with LELANI.

At the end of dance *ENTER* SALLY, unnoticed up-stage C. from L. She looks very blonde against the darkness.

AT END OF MUSIC CUE 15 SEQUE TO

RARATONGA CUE 16

SALLY: Did I disturb you. (*coming down rock piece to centre stage*) I'm sorry. I'll go away. (*Moves*).

MURU: Missie—stay—please!

LELANI: Why-you-not-happy?

SALLY: (*Bravely*) I don't know what you mean—I'm perfectly happy—thank you.

LELANI: Lips-say-smile—but heart-cry-no-happy!

SALLY: Nonsense. We're all having a wonderful time, on Mr. Piggott's yacht.

MURU: Why—why—you not happy? "Raratonga" means "Island of Contented Heart."

SALLY: (*Softly*) Raratonga! Contented Heart. That's a perfect name for this island.

MURU:	You find happiness here, too!
SALLY:	If only I could.
ALL:	You will—you will.

CALL: BUDDY.

MUSIC CUE No. 16. "RARATONGA"

(SALLY and CHORUS)

1 *Refrain, 1 Verse, 2nd Refrain.*

REFRAIN 1.

SALLY AND
VOCAL BACK-
GROUND FROM
CHORUS:

Raratonga ... Raratonga!
　　Lovely land by the lazy lagoon
Raratonga ... Heav'nly garden
　　Bright as gold with the dust of the moon
And no matter where I wander
　　I can never forget if I will
With her necklace of stars and those whisp'ring guitars
　　Raragtonga will be with me still.

VERSE 1.

SALLY:

Geography lessons at school
　　I sat around in a daze,
Hadn't a notion of island or ocean
　　And fluffed all my capes and my bays.
Now there's one magic island, it's plain,
　　Where a part of my heart will remain ...

REFRAIN 2.

ADD VOCAL
BACKGROUND:

Raratonga ... Raratonga!
　　Lovely world by the lazy lagoon.
Raratonga! Heav'nly garden
　　Bright as gold with dust of the moon.
And no matter where you wander
　　You can never forget if you will

SALLY:

With her necklace of stars and those whisp'ring guitars
　　Raratonga will be with me still.

SWITCHBOARD CUE No. 31.

(After " Raratonga " exit ISLANDERS *L. and R.*
Enter BUDDY *L.U.E. down ramp)*

BUDDY:	Hey, Sally, come along. The boys are all ashore from the yacht. Everyone's crazy to get the party started.
SALLY:	You can do without *me.*
BUDDY:	*(Reproachfully)* Now, Sally——: You're pretty unhappy aren't you?
SALLY:	You should talk? Leaving New York with your first show coming on!
BUDDY:	What's left of it!
SALLY:	I'm sick and tired of this, Buddy. The " Pleasure Cruise " is nothing but a floating hotel. It nearly ruined the Van Nordens—and now it's ruining Percy.

BUDDY: You should see him up there (*Gesture to L.*) with the natives—throwing his loot around left and right.

SALLY: Next thing is he'll buy the island. Oh, Buddy, if we could only get him away from here —— ?

BUDDY: (*Hopefully*) Back to New York ?

SALLY: That'd do for a start. Then we could pay off the crew before he fritters away his last few dollars.

BUDDY: We can't *force* him to leave here ... or ... can we ?

SALLY: *Can't* we, Buddy ?

BUDDY: Kidnapping's pretty tough ... !

SALLY: But it's in such a good cause! We'd be saving him from himself.

> The SAILORS *from the yacht come from up left
> —down the rock piece.*

SAILOR: Hi, Buddy! Where's this party ?

BUDDY: (*Suddenly*) Sally! I've got an idea! It *might* work ...

SALLY: What is it ?

BUDDY: Don't ask questions! Get back to the yacht! I'll meet you there in half an hour. And then—oh, boy! New York! And Lilac!!

> SALLY *runs off quickly L.I.E.*

SAILOR 1: I thought you'd finished with all that.

SAILOR 2: Why should you want to go back ?

BUDDY: Because you big lug—I'm still in love with her ! It may be hell—but oh, brother—it's heaven!

CALL: PERCY.

MUSIC CUE No. 17.

> Reprise of " TROUBLE WITH MY HEART."
> (*Sung in waltz time—1 Refrain*)
> BUDDY and BOYS.

BUDDY:
BOYS
 VOCAL BACK-
 GROUND:
Trouble with my heart!
　　　That's what's wrong with me
I've got every single symptom that there can be.
　　　Trembling like a leaf,
Tearful and distrait
　　　I get more of a problem ev'ry day!
On my fever chart
　　　There's an upward curve
Where she smiled at someone else—and I lost my nerve!
　　　Maybe I'm a fool.
Maybe I'm not smart,
　　　But I know that I'm sure of the cure for my trouble-
　　　　　some heart.

BUDDY: (*To* SAILORS) Would you boys do a job for me ?

SAILORS: Sure, Buddy!

BUDDY:	I won't say it's strictly on the level but it's in a darn good cause. I'll make it worth your while.
SAILORS:	We don't want money—we've got plenty. All we want is New York.
BUDDY:	Help me out and you'll be there in a couple of weeks! *(The drums start quietly).*

MUSIC CUE No. 18 " PROCESSION "

	The party's about to start! *(To a sailor)* Get hold of a couple of strong bits of rope!
HANK:	Okay!
BUDDY:	The rest of you guys come along with me-!

BUDDY *and the* SAILORS *EXIT quickly R.2.E.*
SWITCHBOARD CUE No. 32.

No. 18.
*The drums are very loud now, and native boys
and girls enter in procession, garlands round
their necks, down ramp up L.
They are joined by the sailors.
Finally* PERCY *ENTERS, garlanded and
crowned with flowers, from R.3.E. seated on
ceremonial chair carried by sailors, who place
him down stage C.*

CHORUS:	Raratonga! Raratonga! (CHORUS *take positions and sit down).*
PERCY:	I do feel a silly king. I never thought when I came on this pleasure cruise I'd be crowned king of an island. But we're having a champion holiday. *(Rising from chair).*

MUSIC CUE No. 19. " PLEASURE CRUISE "
(PERCY and CHORUS)
1 *Verse,* 1 *Refrain,* 2nd *Verse,* 2nd *Refrain.*
CALL: CAPTAIN AND BUDDY.
VERSE 1.

Holiday time—some sunny clime
Calling to you and me
You quickly choose—a wonderful cruise
Out on the open sea.
The first day you're content
You're awfully glad you went
REFRAIN 1.

On a pleasure cruise—to drive away the blues
The pleasures of a pleasure cruise.
Down the companion way
You fall ten times a day
Someone finds you
Sitting on the point of the captain's compass.

On the deck, you nearly break your neck,
 Your sea legs you can't use
You dive into the ocean for a swim it's such a lark,
 Till you find you've been bitten in the bulwarks
  by a shark,
On a pleasure cruise—to drive away the blues
 The pleasures of a pleasure cruise.

VERSE 2.

ADD CHORUS
Humming:

Steamers and tramps—show coloured lamps,
 Amber and green and red
Your ship runs aground—and somehow you've found
 The street traffic lights instead.
You sail once more then find,
 You've left half the ship behind.

REFRAIN 2.

ADD CHORUS
Singing
Oo—oo:

On a pleasure cruise to drive away the blues
 The pleasures of a pleasure cruise.

PERCY:
Solo

Your cabin's far too small, you've got no room at all
 Someone finds you
Sitting on your bunk with your feet through the porthole.
 One dark night—I turned first left then right
My way I seemed to lose
 A honeymooning couple they created such a scene
Because I was discovered where the bridegroom should
  have been.

ADD CHORUS
Singing
Oo—oo:

On a pleasure cruise—to drive away the blues
 The pleasures of a pleasure cruise.

REFRAIN 3.

UKELELE SOLO.

CHORUS stand and sing on last 8 bars only Oo-ooh.
(Double forte). On last note CHORUS fling arms up
with a " Hey "!

ENCORE: 1 *Refrain* ".SAVING UP FOR SALLY."
   and
 1 *Refrain* " PLEASURE CRUISE "
  2nd *Refrain*—Solo on Uke.

PERCY:

I'm saving up for Sally—
 Saving for a rainy day.
I save what I can spare—a penny here and there.
 And just to keep us off the rocks,
I pop it in my money box.
 Oh I'm not the lad to dally
Of Sally I'm as proud as I can be.
 It's a lovely thing to be her beau
But one thing I should like to know—
 Is Sally saving up a bit for me ?

On the " Pleasure Cruise "—to drive away your blues.
The pleasures of a pleasure cruise.
Down the companion way—you fall ten times a day.
Sally finds me playing pat-a-cake with a girl
In the stoke hole,
On the deck, you nearly break your neck
Your sea legs you can't use.
A girl fell overboard—and was found as sure as fate
With her legs around the lighthouse
And her arms around the mate
Oh, what a pleasure cruise, to drive away your blues
The pleasures of a pleasure cruise.

2nd Refrain " PLEASURE CRUISE " Solo on Uke.
CHORUS sing Oo-ooh—on last two lines.

> *At end of number* PERCY *gives cue by touching
> his wreath of flowers with his right hand—and
> four sailors run forward and pull him into
> ceremonial chair. They tie his arms with ropes
> tied on to the arms of the chair.*

PERCY :   Eh, what's to do ?

HANK :   O.K. Boss—just part of the coronation ceremony.

SAILOR :   We're taking you for a ride! (*The four sailors lift the
             chair*).

MUSIC CUE No. 19B. REPRISE OF
                              " PLEASURE CRUISE "

PERCY :   Oh, are we going for a ta-ta ?

SWITCHBOARD CUE No. 33.

LIGHTS FADE—TABS CLOSE.
END OF SCENE.
DROP IN SCENE 7 CLOTH.

ACT II.
SCENE 7 (Playing Time 4 mins.)
MUSIC FADES AS TABS OPEN
SWITCHBOARD CUE No. 34.
THE SEASHORE.

Characters in this scene:
BUDDY   CAPTAIN   SAILORS

Front cloth scene. BUDDY nervously smoking
ENTERS.
BUDDY and CAPTAIN enter L.1.E.

BUDDY :   Oh, Captain.

CAPTAIN :   I've fixed everything, but I don't like it. I was never
             mixed up with this kind of business before.

BUDDY :   It'll work out, Captain, you see!

| CAPTAIN: | It's all very well for you to talk—you won't have to take the rap! |

CAPTAIN: It's all very well for you to talk—you won't have to take the rap!

BUDDY: There are some things, Captain, we just can't do according to the book . . .

CAPTAIN: I guess you could talk a man into scuttling his own ship. I'm going back on board. Give me a flash when you're all set.

BUDDY: And you'll send the launch ?

CAPTAIN: I guess so—but don't be too long—I don't like the look of the weather.

EXIT L.1.E.

BUDDY: You won't regret it—so long—and thanks a million! Captain—I'll wait here.

SAILORS *ENTER for CHORUS from L.1.E. and R.1.E.*

SAILOR: It's O.K.—it's all fixed—we've got him!

BUDDY: Thanks, fellows—then we're all set for New York.

SAILOR 1: New York ?

SAILOR 2: I'm sick of the darned sea.

BUDDY: I got news for you—I'm sick of the darned sea, too!

CALL: OPERATOR, SALLY, MOTTY, PAULA, VAN NORDEN, PERCY.

MUSIC CUE No. 20:

"RUNNING AWAY TO LAND"
(BUDDY and CHORUS) (*See* DANCE PLOT)

1 *Verse,* 1 *Refrain,* 1 *Couplet,* 2*nd Refrain,* 2*nd Couplet,* 2*nd Verse,* 3*rd Refrain,* 3*rd Couplet,* 4*th Refrain,* 4*th Couplet.*

Verse 1

BUDDY: When I was just a little guy, I used to get a kick,
From reading great adventures 'bout the tale of Moby Dick,
To run away to sea one day—it was my dearest vow
But after a life on the rollin' main,
You ought to see me now!

SWITCHBOARD CUE No. 35.

Refrain 1

BUDDY: I'm running away to land—that's where I long to be
Gimme the life that I adore—the rollicking reckless life ashore—
The kick of the city streets. Adventure everywhere—
Lemme get back to Brooklyn where a man can do or dare.

E

Couplet 1

BUDDY: I'm longing for romance, and spoilin' for a fight
But I'd love to be back when the Dodgers win on a really dirty night.
I've wandered around the world—to every coral strand,
Anyone else can have the sea—I'm running away to land.

Refrain 2

BUDDY
& CHORUS: I'm running away to land—that's where I long to be
Gimme the life that I adore—the rollicking reckless life ashore—
The kick of the city streets—adventure everywhere,
Lemme get back to Brooklyn where a man can do or dare.

Couplet 2

BUDDY: The romance of the deep, that's just a lot of junk.
I'm sick of the movies every night, with my breakfast in my bunk.
I've wandered around the world—to every coral strand.
Anyone else can have the sea—I'm running away to land.

Verse 2

BUDDY: A nautical existence is monotonous and tame
A million mile of ocean , and it's all of it the same.
The ships are air conditioned, there's a lift to go aloft.
No running away to sea for me, it's cissy and it's soft.

Refrain 3

BUDDY: I'm running away to land, the only place for me.
Let me get back to shore again
Where women are dolls—and men are men,
Sick of the Southern Lights—fed up with flying fish.
Every time I think of home, I cross my eyes and wish.

Couplet 3

BUDDY: A wife in every port—they told me was the life
But I'd rather be back in a cocktail bar—
With a port in every wife
I've travelled the briny blue—but kindly understand
Anyone else can have the sea—I'm running away to land.

CLOSE TABS

Refrain 4

BOYS: I'm running away to land. The only place for me.
Let me get back to shore again—where women are dolls and men are men
Sick of the Southern Lights—fed up with flying fish
Every time I think of home—I cross my eyes and wish.

Couplet 4

BUDDY: Here's to old New York—we'll greet her with a grin—
To hell with a life on the ocean wave
Leave that to Errol Flynn.

BUDDY
& CHORUS: I've travelled the briny blue

BUDDY: But kindly understand—anyone else can have the sea.

BOYS: Anyone else can have the sea

BUDDY
& BOYS: I'll ... Go ... Back ... To ...
Running away, running away, running away, running away.

BUDDY
& BOYS: Land .....
We'll ... go .. back ... to ... land.

SWITCHBOARD CUE No. 36.

BLACK OUT ON END OF NUMBER

ACT II.
SCENE 8A (Playing Time: 10 mins.)
SWITCHBOARD CUE No. 37.

MUSIC CUE 20A. SEGUE. "RUNNING AWAY TO LAND"

Open tabs as soon as BUDDY and 2 SAILORS are in Cabin.
ON BOARD THE "PLEASURE CRUISE."

Characters in this scene:

BUDDY	WIRELESS OPERATOR
2 SAILORS	VAN NORDEN
SALLY	PAULA
MOTTY	PERCY

Composite set framed in a cut out, consisting of:—

(a) *The Owner's Cabin* (*R*).
Luxuriously appointed little stateroom. Door at back to deck. Wardrobe at back L. of door. Bunk L. Picture hanging over bunk L. One wicker armchair R.C. 1 shelf on L. side of wardrobe, with whisky bottle and three glasses on it. Communicating archway to wireless cabin, Centre. One shelf above door, with life-belt on it. One Indian rug on floor.

(b) *The Wireless Cabin* (*L*).
Smaller room with radio desk with wireless unit R. (headphones, morse tapper, red and green lights). Lamp in right corner. Loudspeaker on wall. Chair for operator R.
When the tabs open, Operator is seated at radio desk, reading a magazine and listening to weather report. In stateroom TWO SAILORS are having a quick drink with BUDDY.

ANNOUNCER OVER MIKE:	Calling Motor Yacht " Pleasure Cruise " Calling Motor Yacht " Pleasure Cruise " Your message received . . . Here is your weather report . . . Wind westerly—reaching gale force before midnight. Over!

MUSIC FADES OUT.

BUDDY: Okay, fellers, a fine job. Thanks a lot.

SAILORS: A pleasure, Mr. Delany!
Goodnight, sir! Oh, what shall we do with his clothes ?
(Picks up and displays bundle of PERCY'S *clothes).*

BUDDY: Put 'em in the slop-chest. Goodnight, boys.
With a half-salute and a wink, EXIT SAILORS
*L. As they go through cabin—ENTER from
deck, back of set,* SALLY *and* MOTTY.

MOTTY: *(Grumbling indignantly)* One minute we're on shore—
next we're sent back to ship—my head's beginning to
go round like a tee-to-tum! *(Sitting on chair R.)*

SALLY: Don't worry, Dad. *(Sitting on down stage end of bunk).*
(Anxiously) Is everybody on board, Buddy ?

BUDDY: Everything's under control. *(Thumbs up).*

MOTTY: *(Who has been staring)* What *is* all this ? What are you
kids talking about ?

BUDDY: *(Patting his shoulder)* You'll find out, Mr. Whittle.
(Crossing to R.) Hank, Mr. Piggott gave me this—it's
a message for his office in New York.

OPERATOR: *(Reading wire)* " Am sailing tonight . . . " but the
weather report isn't too good, Mr. Delany . . .

BUDDY: Forget the weather—send that off at once.

MOTTY: *(Startled)* What's that—sailing ?

OPERATOR: *(Scribbling)* Sailing tonight . . . expect dock New York
around December twentieth. Will cable full instructions
later. Regards. Piggott.

BUDDY: All correct. Shoot that off right away! *(Gives tip).*

OPERATOR: You bet! *(Pockets tip).* Thanks, Mr. Delany.

MOTTY: *(Rising)* Buddy, I demand an explanation!

BUDDY: I've got to see the Captain and get the anchor moving.
So long, Sally. *(Exits through door R. at back).*
OPERATOR *begins to send message.*

MOTTY: What's going on ? You're getting me properly
flummoxed!

SALLY: It's perfectly simple, Dad. We're leaving the island
tonight—and in fourteen days we'll be in New York!

MOTTY: A bit sudden, isn't it ? Are these Percy's orders ?

SALLY: We—ell . . . no.

MOTTY:	Then whose are they?
SALLY:	Captain O'Sullivan's.
MOTTY:	(*Anxiously*) But what's Percy got to say to all this?
SALLY:	We didn't ask him.
MOTTY:	You didn't? But supposing Percy won't leave?
SALLY:	Don't worry, he will. We're sailing right away.
MOTTY:	You're glad?
SALLY:	For Percy's sake—yes.
MOTTY:	Lass—you're worrying about that Paula!
SALLY:	(*Not very convincingly*) Oh, no, I'm not!
MOTTY:	Yes, you are. You've got the Whittle pride. But don't let pride beat you, Lass. He'll come to his senses—and when he *does*—see that you're waiting for him!
SALLY:	(*Moved*) Bless you, love. You know, you're a champion Father for a girl to have!
MOTTY:	(*Modestly*) Well, I *try*, you know. But you being the only one, I never had much *practice*!

            ENTER VAN NORDEN *and* PAULA *through cabin door L. They stare with distaste at* MOTTY *and* SALLY.

VAN NORDEN:	What's the meaning of all this?
PAULA:	Where's Percy?
VAN NORDEN:	Who gave orders for this yacht to sail?
MOTTY:	Orders? Who should give orders—the *owner*, I expect!
SALLY:	This *is* Percy's yacht, you know.
PAULA:	I am aware of that, but where is he?
MOTTY:	To tell you the truth, I don't rightly know.
PAULA:	Perhaps you can inform us, Miss Whittle?
SALLY:	Not at this moment, Miss Van Norden. Come on, Dad, let's splice the mainbrace. (SALLY *exit through door L. at back*).
MOTTY:	Aye, aye, Cap'n. Shiver me timbers—yo-ho—and a bottle of rum.

            MOTTY *EXITS through door L. at back to deck hilariously.*

VAN NORDEN:	Now what was all that about?
PAULA:	They're up to something. I never did care for that little...
VAN NORDEN:	(*Shrugging it off, sitting on bunk L.*) My dear Paula, the child's just a *nobody*!
PAULA:	They're all nobodies, the whole pack of 'em—and (*viciously*) that goes for Percy Piggott, too!
VAN NORDEN:	(*Anxiously*) My dear, you're not going sour on him?

PAULA:	What do you expect me to do? Run round after him doing the Dance of the Seven Veils? (*Sits on chair R.*)
VAN NORDEN:	He may not be out of the top drawer, but I have him interested in a couple of projects...
PAULA:	Oh, to hell with your projects! I'm sick of them *and* Percy Piggott!
VAN NORDEN:	(*Aggrieved*) Right now things are pretty tight on Wall Street...
PAULA:	And so I can make a fool of myself in front of all my friends?
VAN NORDEN:	I don't get you...
PAULA:	You don't get anything—not even the cracks I've put up with since I started going around with this dumb dope!
VAN NORDEN:	Piggott's a shrewd young man...
PAULA:	*Shrewd?* Father, be your age!
VAN NORDEN:	How about United Fertilizer?
PAULA:	Sucker's luck! If Percy wasn't half-witted, he wouldn't listen to the stuff *you're* feeding him!
VAN NORDEN:	(*Hotly*) I resent that!
	Knock on wardrobe.
	Come in!! All I ask is a little help.
PAULA:	Little help—such as *what*?
	Knock on wardrobe.
VAN NORDEN:	Come in.
PAULA:	—Marrying the poor sap?
VAN NORDEN:	(*Acting shocked*) *Paula!* Really!
PAULA:	Oh, don't put on that pious expression! I know where all those newspaper blurbs came from—and I tell you I don't care for it!
	Knock on wardrobe.
VAN NORDEN:	Come in! (*Truculently*) So you don't huh?
PAULA:	(*Angry and almost shouting*) And let me tell you something else. I'd do most things, but I wouldn't marry your Mr. Piggott—not if he was the last man on earth and we were starving in the gutter!
	Knock on wardrobe.
BOTH & OPERATOR:	Come in!!!
	The wardrobe door flies open and flat onto the stateroom floor between them falls PERCY, *clad in nothing but a set of woollen combinations, black socks and suspenders.* *He has a white handkerchief tied over his mouth.*

VAN NORDEN: Why, Mr. Piggott!
PAULA: Percy!
PERCY: (*Scrambing to his feet, helped by Van Norden, who takes handkerchief from mouth, with dignity*) Good evening! Delighted to see you folks, it's me, Percy Piggott, the goomp—the *dope* ... The sap.

> PERCY, *with great dignity goes over R. takes yachting cap off peg, puts it on head as he crosses, EXITING R. Cabin door.*

...Good morning, all.

VAN NORDEN: (*Going to door D.R. and holding it open. To* PAULA, *angrily*) A million dollars thrown in the air, because you can't keep your mouth shut.

PAULA: (*Now calm*) Well, at least he heard the truth.

VAN NORDEN: (*Furious*) The truth ? What's good in telling him the truth ? Did you ever hear *me* tell the truth ?

PAULA: (*Sweetly*) Never—intentionally.

VAN NORDEN: (*Still furious*) Oh, really, Paula.

> They both exit L. door of cabin.
> PERCY pops his head round cabin door R.

PERCY: 'Ave they gone ?

CALL: LILAC, SINGERS, DANCERS.

OPERATOR: Yes.

PERCY: (*Shivering bus.*) 'Ell of a draught coming from some-where. I don't know where it's coming from, but I know where it's going to! Have you got something I could slip on ? (OPERATOR *hands* PERCY *pair of shorts*). Help yourself to a drink. (OPERATOR *pours out a drink for himself and* PERCY). (PERCY *sits in chair;* OPERATOR *sits on bunk*). Well it's been a day, hasn't it ? The lads have had a bit of fun with me, haven't they ? First I'm crowned king of an island, then I'm kidnapped and put in there, an what about them two who were here just now ? The things they were saying in front of my face behind my back! Sometimes I wish I were on a train going back to Newton-Le-Willows.

OPERATOR: I guess you've got some pretty good railways in England.

PERCY: Oh, yes, we've got some good railways in England, but something funny's been 'appening to 'em lately. I don't know whether you'd really understand over here. They've what you call—Nationalised them—what they've really done—is—*Paralysed them.* But we were talking about Newton-Le-Willows (*Puts down drink*). It's a pretty little place surrounded by a lot of coal pits; you know what coal pits are, don't you ? There's a big wheel with a pulley and this lets down little tubs which bring up the coal and empty it into goods wagons;

then these wagons are *whisked* away—well—they're not *whisked* exactly (*demonstrates speed of wagon with hand*). After that we don't know what happens to the coal, *we* never see any of it. These coal wagons are going backwards and forwards—give me a pencil, I,ll show you what I mean.

OPERATOR *hands* PERCY *a pencil.*

PERCY *commences to draw on cupboard door with the following commentary:—*

First we have a railway line going down like this

then one going across like this

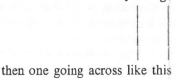

Now its two miles from there (A) to there (A) and two miles from there (B) to there (B). Up here (A) we have the 5.55 Goods train leaving at approximately 5.55 and over here (B) we have the 6 o'clock leaving at 6 o'clock. Over here we have a signal box——

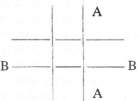

Over here we have a wooden hut——

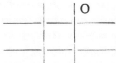

and here we have a little cottage——

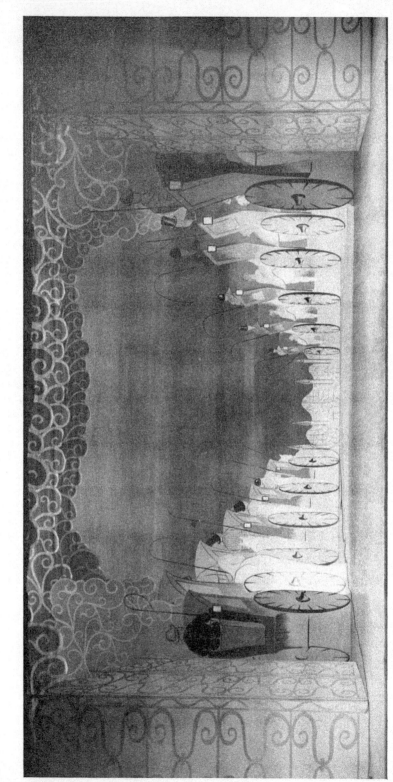

"GARTER GIRL."—Full Set.

Act 2 : Sc. 8(b).

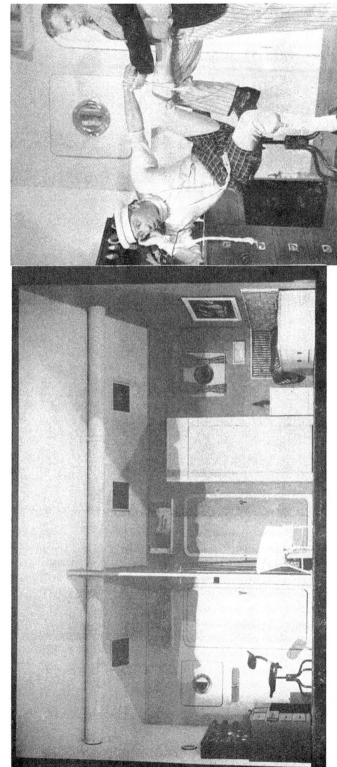

'Percy' radios the all-important message.
Act 2 : Sc. 8(c).

Act 2 : Sc. 8(a) & 8(c).   ON BOARD THE PLEASURE CRUISE.
All doors, including cupboard, practical.

and over here is Newton-Le-Willows Station——

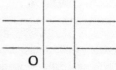

O

There's the platform and oh, they've put a seat on it now.

Well, one Wednesday afternoon—or was it a Thursday ? No, it was Wednesday, I remember now because my Aunt Fanny had her operation on the Monday. Well this Wednesday afternoon the man in the signal box got a very important message, and when he got it, something happened to him because he rushed out of the signal box, jumped over that line and that line and went into that little hut where he grabbed a big pickaxe; then he chopped his way out and chopped over that line and over that line and chopped his way into that little cottage. Now in that cottage there was a poor old man who was very very ill. Oh, he was bad, they'd been poulticing him for six months. Well, he wrapped the old man in a blanket and then picked him up and chopped his way out of the cottage over that line and over that line and laid the poor old man on the seat here. The old man looked up and said, " What's to do ? " " Well," said the man from the signal box, " I've just had a very important message to say that the 5.55 is going to be five minutes late, so if you lie there and watch there, you'll see the finest bloody train smash you've ever seen in your life!

(BUZZER and FLASH from radio set)

ANNOUNCER: *(On mike in audience)* *(As* OPERATOR *fiddles with tuning, MUSIC grows louder and voice of Announcer heard over it).*

This is Station W-J-Zee, New York City. Tonight we present a ring-side broadcast—a hook-up from the stage of the Ziegfeld Theatre—an excerpt from the world premiere of the fabulous Percy Piggott musical " Garter Girl " (PERCY *quickly pours a drink*)—starring Lilac Lamore!

MUSIC CUE No. 21. " GARTER GIRL "

OPERATOR: Mr. Piggott—quickly—the radio—it's New York—it's from the Ziegfeld Theatre—get a load of this—its that show of yours! Starring Lilac Lamore!

PERCY: What's the date ?

OPERATOR: December six.

PERCY: December sixth ? Holy Smoke! It's the opening night of my new show.

OPERATOR:	I can bring her in better'n that. You're going to enjoy this, Mr. Piggott!
PERCY:	I am an' all—if it's as lousy as I hope it is going to be.

CLOSE TABS.

ANNOUNCER:	Ladies and Gentlemen—" The Garter Girl."

QUICK FADE OUT.

SWITCHBOARD CUE No. 38.

MUSIC CUE No. 21A " THE GARTER GIRL "

(LILAC, SINGERS AND DANCERS)

ACT II.

SCENE 8B (Playing Time: 5 mins.)

SWITCHBOARD CUE No. 39.

" THE GARTER GIRL " (*See Dance Plot*)

CALL: ANNOUNCER, PERCY, MOTTY, SALLY, BUDDY, OPERATOR, CAPTAIN, VAN NORDEN.

Characters in this scene:
> LILAC
> SINGERS AND DANCERS
>> The number starts on Tabs. opening on to full set. At cue the Tabs close, and the number finishes in front of Tabs.
>> TO OPEN—The girls enter from stage R. and L. on musical introduction.

REFRAIN 1.

MEN SINGING THROUGH PROMPT CORNER MIKE:	The Garter Girl............ The Garter Girl............ She's going to Delmonico's To dance! Dance! Dance with Diamond Jim.

MIKE OFF AT END.

SWITCHBOARD CUE No. 40.

> The girls continue movement in front of tabs until the end of the first refrain of " The Garter Girl." The swagged tabs open four bars before the end of the first refrain of " The Garter Girl " revealing LILAC C. with boys in a crowd around her. The picture is held for the fanfare. Then LILAC walks down stage on four bars.
>
> Introduction to first verse of " The Garter Girl."

VERSE 1.

LILAC: You must have heard a rumour that I'd got into town
From Caribou to Uma, they've heard of my renown.
The girl who's got the garter, who weakens now and then
A lady who's a martyr to the wicked thoughts of men.

BOYS: It must be swell to be a loving wife.

LILAC: (But a diamond garter lasts for all your life).

SWITCHBOARD CUE No. 41.

REFRAIN 2.

BOYS: The Garter Girl! The Garter Girl!

LILAC: The town belongs to me.

BOYS: You'll never find a smarter girl. Wherever you may be.

LILAC: If Mr. Astor telephones—my kind regards to him.
I'm going to Delmonico's to dance with Diamond Jim.

BOYS: She's going to Delmonico's to dance with Diamond Jim.

REFRAIN 3.

BOYS & The Garter Girl! The Garter Girl!
GIIRLS: With music she's " Au fait "
Although she's no sonata girl—A Polka tune's O.K.
Her slipper will be filled tonight with clicquot to the brim.
She's going to Delmonico's to dance with Diamond Jim
She' s going to Delmonico's to dance with Diamond Jim.

This refrain is followed by—

16 bars " Offenbach Music "

6 bars Tacet

2 bars Piano Solo

8 First bars of Refrain of " The Garter Girl " which the boys whistle

4 bars Offenbach Music

(LILAC *exits with four dancing boys during this. L.1.E.*)

28 bars (i.e. refrain and a half of " The Garter Girl ")

LILAC re-enters R.3.E. after 8 bars and dances down stage C. Four boys raise her up on sticks for picture.

(A large garter comes down from flys on last 4 bars—in front of LILAC)

Hold picture for applause.

(*Close tabs.*)

Encore of " THE GARTER GIRL "

6 bars introduction into 2nd verse.

(LILAC *is lowered down to stage by boys. The garter is also lowered from 1st dead, to stage level during 6 bars introduction).*

VERSE 2.

LILAC: That certain Mr. Brady who's known as Diamond Jim Knows how to treat a lady,

BOYS: If she looks good to him!
At Tiffany's one morning—he spied upon the shelf A great big diamond garter—

LILAC: (And he fitted it himself).

BOYS: And that is how she got herself the name—

LILAC: That makes Madame La Pompadour look tame.

REFRAIN 5.

BOYS &
GIIRLS: The Garter Girl! The Garter Girl!
To-morrow she'll be wed. She'll be an upper strata girl—
Respectable—but dead!
We guess it will be beautiful—but in the interim,
She's going to Delmonico's,
To dance—dance—dance with Diamond Jim.

HOLD PICTURE FOR APPLAUSE.

BLACK OUT.

SWITCHBOARD CUE No. 42.

Boys and girls exit stage L. and R. LILAC exits stage R.

Orchestra repeat refrain of " The Garter Girl " until tabs open on to Scene 8c.

ACT II.

SCENE 8c (Playing Time: 6 mins.)

SWITCHBOARD CUE No. 43.

ON BOARD THE " PLEASURE CRUISE "
(*Same as* SCENE 8A)

Characters in this scene:

ANNOUNCER	BUDDY
PERCY	CAPTAIN
MOTTY	WIRELESS OPERATOR
SALLY	VAN NORDEN

As the TABS open and lights come up, broadcast in finishing.

BUDDY is listening with SALLY and MOTTY beside him. OPERATOR in cabin is listening, too. Applause is faded to background as ANNOUNCER speaks, PERCY is sitting in complete dejection on chair R. of stateroom.

ANNOUNCER :	This Ziegfeld Theatre audience is going *crazy*!
SALLY :	(*Thrilled*) Dad, do listen!
MOTTY :	By gum, the lad's done it!
ANNOUNCER :	Yes, sir! " Garter Girl's " here to stay—Lilac Lamore is Broadway's newest and brightest sta*r*.
BUDDY :	(*Excitedly*) She's done it!
ANNOUNCER :	Congratulations go to you, Percival Piggott—wherever you are—" Garter Girl " should make a *million*!
PERCY :	(*Dazed*) What was that ?
ANNOUNCER :	(*Deliberately*) Yes, sir, one million!

> PERCY *does a " take." The broadcast is over. They crowd round him excitedly.*

SALLY :	Don't you understand—your show's a smash hit in New York.
BUDDY :	And you've made Lilac Broadway's newest star—you gave her the break—I always knew she'd make it! Thanks and congratulations.
OPERATOR :	Attaboy, Mr. Piggott. That's quite a bankroll—another million!

> *Deck moves.*

PERCY :	(*Angrily*) But I don't *want* another million! I want a cup of tea!
OTHERS :	*Don't want it ?*

> *Business of exchanging glances.*

BUDDY :	Do you mean you deliberately wanted the show to be a turkey ?
PERCY :	I can't afford it …
MOTTY :	Can't afford it!
BUDDY :	Well, how do you like that!
MOTTY :	(*Sarcastically*) I suppose then if it makes money you'll decide to take the show off ?
PERCY :	That's the idea—Motty—close it up.

> *Deck moves a bit.*

OTHERS :	*Wha—at ?*
PERCY :	(*To* OPERATOR) Young man, you get through to New York, tell Manager at Ziegfeld Theatre—give all *of 'em in show a fortnight's notice*! And a month's salary.
OPERATOR :	B-but, Mr. Piggott, you can't do that …
PERCY :	(*Violently*) You do as I tell you—and quick!
PERCY :	Yes, sir … (*Turns to go*).
BUDDY :	Wait a minute.

> OPERATOR *hesitates.* BUDDY *is now in command of the situation, standing with his back to wireless unit.*

(*Almost threatening*) I've put up with plenty from you

	—but when it comes to cold-bloodedly wrecking the career of a girl who's just made it in a big way ... Boy, I've got a flash for you!

PERCY: And what are you going to *do* about it ?

BUDDY: (*Picking up brass lamp*) Smash that radio so small you you won't even find the pieces! (*Turns to go*).

PERCY: (*Grabbing* BUDDY'S *arm*) Here, here, wait a minute ... (*Holding him*) By gum—he's a well built lad!! (*Boat lurches to left*).

BUDDY: (*Viciously*) You dare do anything to Lilac an you'll see.
There is a tense situation with BUDDY'S *fist raised.*

SALLY: (*At same time as above speech*) Buddy, be careful!

MOTTY: (*At same time as above speech*) Take it easy, lads!
A peal of thunder, rushing of wind—and the deck heaves more.

SALLY: (*Scared*) My goodness, whatever's that ?

OPERATOR: A storm coming up ? Captain's been expecting it ...

MOTTY: (*Tremously*) Thunder and lightning ? Open all the windows.
Boat rocks. More thunder.

PERCY: Don't worry, Motty—Sally love—we're all right, anchored safe and sound in lagoon!
Boat rocks.
NOTE.—From now onwards till end of scene thunder and wind as directed. Also movement of ship increasing in violence.

OPERATOR: (*Shouting*) But, Mr. Piggott, we're out *at sea*!

PERCY: (*Incredulously*) At sea ?

OPERATOR: We sailed out past the reef half an hour ago.

PERCY: Oh, that's why they locked me in the cupboard! Mutiny eh? Flotsam and Jetsam on the high seas! Did *you* give them orders, Motty ? (*Moving to* MOTTY *L.C.*)

SALLY: (*Cutting in*) Dad knew nothing about it, Percy. *I* gave them.

PERCY: (*Looking surprised*) You ?

BUDDY: She did not. If you want to pick on somebody—pick on me!

PERCY: You're too big.

SALLY: We couldn't bear to see you losing all your money on the island ...

BUDDY: (*Cutting in*) So Mr. Piggott, you're on your way to New York!

PERCY:	(*Brokenly*) Three weeks till January first. Oh, Sally, Sally, you don't know what you've done to me. (*Sits on chair R.*)
	CAPTAIN *bursts in from deck L. cabin door.*
CAPTAIN:	Mr. Piggott. I don't like the look of things ...
PERCY:	And *I* don't like the feel of them either!
CAPTAIN:	There's a gale blowing up. We may be in trouble by morning!
PERCY:	By morning? (*Rising*) You're going to be in trouble tonight!
CAPTAIN:	What?
PERCY:	Captain, who gave you orders to sail this ship?
CAPTAIN:	I thought ...
PERCY:	(*Cutting in violently*) You thought—who's the owner of this yacht?
CAPTAIN:	You sir, but ...
PERCY:	Then turn round and get back to the island, quick.
CAPTAIN:	Turn round? In weather like this?
PERCY:	I don't care about weather—you do as I say and get back!
MOTTY:	(*Wailing*) What are you trying to do, Percy—drown us all?
CAPTAIN:	We're only just clear of the big reef, sir ...
PERCY:	Well, if you can't clear it—take the blasted thing with you. You've had your orders, Captain—*obey 'em*!
	Ship lurches deeply to R.
	PERCY *salutes and falls backwards into chair.*
CAPTAIN:	Very good, sir—but don't blame me—you're the owner. (*Clicks his heels and turns to* OPERATOR) Operator, you'd better stick mighty close to that radio!
OPERATOR:	Aye, aye, Cap'n!
	Exit L. cabin door.
SALLY:	Percy, you must be out of your mind!
PERCY:	But, Sally, if I get back to New York—I'm ruined.
MOTTY:	While you're busy being ruined, I'm going to have a look at lifeboats! Come on, Sally.
	They Exit L. Cabin door.
	Thunder—wind—ship heaves more violently. *Silent business of* PERCY *walking up and down in despair.* *Finally sitting on bunk—under picture.*
CAPTAIN:	(*Off*) Put out the deck lights!
VOICES:	(*Off*) Aye, aye, sir!
CAPTAIN:	(*Off*) Secure all boats! Stand by to rig the storm sail..
VOICES:	(*Off*) Aye, aye, sir!

	ENTER from deck R. cabin door VAN NORDEN.
VAN NORDEN:	(*Furious*) Piggott! Piggott! What's going on? Captain says you've ordered the boat back to the island.
PERCY:	And what if I have? It's my ship.
VAN NORDEN:	In this weather? Are you out of your mind? You don't know these waters.
PERCY:	No, but I'm beginning to learn them damn fast.
VAN NORDEN:	You crazy fool! (*Exit L. Cabin door*).

Ship lurches deeply to right.
EXIT.
There is a splintering crash. Ship pitches.
Picture falls from wall over PERCY'S *head.*

PERCY:	(*Staggering*) Blimey, what was *that*?
OPERATOR:	(*Staggering through door*) Steering gear's gone by the sound of it. (*Staggers back to radio and signals*).

ENTER MOTTY *from deck left cabin door in life jacket.*

MOTTY:	Percy, we've struck the reef!
PERCY:	The damn fool I told him to take it with him!

MUSIC CUE No. 22 " STORM MUSIC "

to end of scene.

MOTTY:	The Captain says blasted rudder's gone. We're going round in circles!
PERCY:	In circles? Motty, you don't mean it?

They both stagger round in a circle—and MOTTY *exits left cabin door banging door in* PERCY'S *face.*
PERCY *stands for a while leaning on door, then staggers to chair C. sits—feels under chair for something to be sick in, then crawls on hands and knees to the Bunk R. as the ship heaves heavily to the left. He opens drawer in the underneath of bunk—then ⸢pretends to be sick in it—closes drawer and crawls back to chair centre as the ship lurches heavily to right. He collapses on chair.*

OPERATOR:	(*Excitedly*) Hey, Mr. Piggott, there's a ship calling us.
PERCY:	Oh, let me die!
OPERATOR:	She's answering my signal—about two miles off our port bow. She asks if we want to be taken in tow!

Re-enter MOTTY.

PERCY:	She does? (*Jumping up*) Then tell her " Yes "!
MOTTY:	But, Percy, we don't need a tow ... Captain's fixed rudder. He says he can get the yacht back to New York in four weeks.

PERCY:	Four weeks? That's no good to me. (*Moves to* OPERATOR) Young man, tell 'em we'll have the best tow they've got!
OPERATOR:	But, Mr. Piggott, the salvage...?
PERCY:	Salvage? What's that?
MOTTY:	He means they'll want paying for it!
OPERATOR:	You bet, sir. And they'll charge you half the value of this yacht.
PERCY:	(*His eyes gleaming*) And will I have to pay the money?
OPERATOR:	Maritime Law, sir!
PERCY:	(*Thrilled*) Then what are we waiting for?
MOTTY:	This yacht is worth five hundred thousand dollars!
PERCY:	Aye, and half that's *two hundred and fifty thousand*! Let me get at that wireless. (*Pushing* OPERATOR *out of chair and sitting on it*).
MOTTY:	He'll be ruined!
OPERATOR:	(*With a shrug*) Owner's orders, sir...
PERCY:	Aye, this is owner giving them. Percy Piggott. What's that?
MOTTY:	Fetch the Captain! (OPERATOR *exits cabin door R.*)
	(*Staggers through to radio,* PERCY *pushes him away.* MOTTY *seizes* PERCY.)
	(*Angrily*) You come away from that!
	MOTTY *catches hold of* PERCY'S *leg*—PERCY *kicks him and* MOTTY *staggers backwards.*)
PERCY:	Mind your own interference! (*Pushing* MOTTY *violently*)
	With the roll of the ship MOTTY *reels back through door into the stateroom.*
PERCY:	(*Resuming operations*) Hello. Hello. This is me! Is that you? Well what have got in the way of tows? Well, have you got one for 250,000 dollars—oh, all right —I'll make it 300,000. That's all the money I've got— after that I'm broke. O.K. come and get us! (*As an afterthought*) Oh, I say—I'll pay for the rope!
	As PERCY *takes his headphones off with a satisfied smile, he sees* MOTTY *looking at him aghast.*
MOTTY:	So you've done it.
PERCY:	Aye, and if I turn my back, you'll *undo* it?
MOTTY:	I will and all.
PERCY:	Well, you won't see. (*He picks up ship's lamp*).
MOTTY:	Percy, what are you going to do?
PERCY:	What I stopped Buddy doing.

F

*He raises ship's lamp to smash radio as a loud
explosion happens back stage R. and flash
from radio panel.*

BLACK OUT.

SWITCHBOARD CUE No. 44.

Draw Tabs.

MUSIC CUE No. 22A " ZIP GOES A MILLION "

END OF SCENE.

ACT II.

SCENE 9 (Playing Time: 4 mins.)

SWITCHBOARD CUE No. 45.

NEW YORK   (TABS)

CALL: PORTERS, PERCY, KELLY, SALLY, MOTTY, BUDDY,
LILAC, PAULA, SINGERS, DANCERS.

Characters in this scene:

BUDDY

LILAC

In darkness through loudspeakers we hear
the NEWSBOYS, cued in with dramatic
treatment of " Zip " music.

No. 22A. MUSICAL LINK—NEWSBOY'S VOICE
OVER MIKE.

NEWSBOYS ·   Paper! Paper! New Year's Sensation! ...

THROUGH   All about the Piggott Crash!

PROMPT   Millionaire playboy to quit Broadway!

CORNER MIKE: Piggott sold up!

MUSIC FADES OUT.

ENTER R. LILAC *in evening gown ...walking
quickly, lost in thought ...and L.* BUDDY
*walking quickly, lost in newspaper. They
almost collide.*

LILAC: *(Joyfully) Buddy!* Gee it's good to see you!

BUDDY: *(A little stiffly)* Happy New Year ... Miss Lamore!

LILAC: Miss Lamore *nothing!* When did you get back ?

BUDDY: Oh, just in time for *(showing paper) the Big Crash!*

LILAC: I know, poor Percy Piggott.

BUDDY: Kind of tough for *you,* too ?

LILAC: *(Misunderstanding)* But didn't you hear Billy Rose
bought the show—we're running on just the same.

BUDDY: I didn't mean that exactly. I was thinking of you and
your screwball boy friend ...

LILAC: Boy friend ?

BUDDY:	Yeah, his shopping days are over!
LILAC:	(*Pretending indignation*) Are you suggesting, Mr. Delany, that there was ever anything between Percy and me ?
BUDDY:	(*With a shrug*) Just a couple of fur coats!
LILAC:	How dumb can an intelligent character be ? Don't you know he belongs to Sally ?
BUDDY:	He has a darned funny way of showing it.
LILAC:	Well, he's a darned funny character. Very like you really.
BUDDY:	Like me!
LILAC:	Of course, honey. *You* picked the girl you wanted— and you're going to get her!
BUDDY:	(*Wide-eyed*) I *am* ?
LILAC:	Sure, you big lug, right now. (*Kisses him*).

MUSIC 23 Segues to Intro. to Duet.

BUDDY:	(*Awed*) Yippee, what a New Year's present!

No. 23. " THOU ART FOR ME."

(BUDDY and LILAC)

1 *Verse*, 1 *Refrain*, 2nd *Refrain* and 6 *Bars Tag*.

VERSE 1.

BUDDY:	Babe, I'm so in love with you it drives me nearly frantic I've so much to say to you (and all of it romantic)
LILAC:	I'm all starry-eyed like any kid ‚So I'll say my piece in Poetry the way **that** Shakespeare did !

REFRAIN 1.

Shall I compare thee to a summer's day !
    A diamond clip, a Rolls coupe ?
Or, baby, shall I simply say
    " Thou art okay ? "

BUDDY:	Shall I compare thee to a flow'ry copse ?
	    A brand-new line in soda-pops ?
	Or murmur as my heart-beat stops
	    " Thou art the tops ? "

LILAC:	Dear heart . . . as a swain Thou couldst hardly be sweller! Thou art my lord and my love . . . my guy, **my** feller!
BUDDY:	Shall I compare thee to a ship at sea ? A rose in bloom ? A symphony ?
LILAC:	Just say that in a high degree " Thou art for me ? "

84

REFRAIN 2.

BUDDY: Shall I compare thee to a dawn in Spring?
A straight in spades from Nine to King?
Or, sweetie, shall I simply sing
"Thou hast that thing?"

LILAC: Shall I compare Thee to a Broadway Show?
A ruby ring? A new chapeau?
Or whisper with that well-known glow
"Thou art my beau?"

BUDDY: Forsooth...as they said in the days of Lord Burleigh
In truth...thou gettest me down both late and early.

LILAC: Shall I compare Thee to a honey-bee?
A bearer-cheque for twenty G.?
Or say that in a high degree
"Thou art for me?"

BUDDY: Pretty baby, Thou are def'nitely for Me!

SWITCHBOARD CUE No. 46.

FADE OUT on end of duet. In darkness ANNOUNCER *speaks over loudspeakers with background of crowd effects. MUSIC behind.*

MUSIC CUE No. 23A. "ZIP GOES A MILLION."

SEGUE. FADE ON OPENING OF TABS.

ANNOUNCER: It's New Year's Eve in Manhattan, folks—nearly the end of another dramatic twelvemonth—and Broadway is packed as only Broadway can be with a milling crowd of revellers waiting for those midnight chimes to say "Let the party go!" And away beyond the bright lights —in every little home and apartment—there'll be a party of one kind or another, too—for this is everybody's celebration—

SWITCHBOARD CUE No. 47.

OPEN TABS—MUSIC FADES.

an evening that can be summed up in the good old traditional phrase—"Happy New Year!"
During broadcast tabs have been drawn back and on the final words F.O.H. LIMES FADE UP on Scene X.

ACT II.

SCENE 10 (Playing Time: 9 mins.)

THE PIGGOTT PENTHOUSE.

Characters in this scene:

PORTERS, PERCY, KELLY, LILAC, SALLY, CONNELLY, MOTTY, BUDDY, SINGERS AND DANCERS.

A beautiful lofty room with a wide spread of windows up stage. For the moment curtains shut out a night-scene of mid-town Manhattan. The room has several doors and a pair of double doors. It has been more or less stripped of furniture and fittings. Centre stage one crate plainly marked SOLD. The room has a desolate air.

When the tabs open PERCY is discovered sitting on crate centre with a large bundle of bills in his lap. He is wearing his First Act suit, the reach-me-downs in which he first arrived in Piggottsville.

(*As tabs open* KELLY *enters up-stage L. and switches on lights.* ENTER *two porters up-stage L.*)

1ST PORTER:	Excuse me, sir.
PERCY:	Don't worry about me lads. (*He rises and puts bundle on mantelpiece and exits R.1.E.*)

The Porters take out crate L.2.E.

KELLY:	There they are, Mr. Piggott, sir. (*Hands* PERCY *thick envelope*) Three passports—three steamer tickets.
PERCY:	Quarter to twelve! I'm much oblige to you, Kelly. (*Takes off wrist-watch*) This'll settle things. I'd like *you* to have this. (*Gives watch*).
KELLY:	I'd rather not, Mr. Piggott. It's been a real pleasure . . .
PERCY:	You'll be doing *me* a real pleasure.
KELLY:	Well, thanks, sir, and goodbye.
PERCY:	(*Happily*) Nay, not " good-bye." I might be back—you never know.

MUSIC CUE No. 24. " ORDINARY PEOPLE "

(*Reprise 8 Bars*)

EXIT *very happily R.1.E.*

KELLY *looks admiringly at the watch and is about to exit by double doors when* SALLY ENTERS *L.2.E. in her First Act Runcorn dress.*

KELLY:	Good evening, miss. Shall I tell Mr. Piggott you're here ?
SALLY:	No thank you, I'll wait.

KELLY EXITS *L.2.E.* SALLY *looks round the denuded room rather bleakly.*

ENTER PERCY, *carrying the hat and mackintosh in which he arrived first from Runcorn. Still humming, he sets them down neatly on top of handbag upstage R. in front of fireplace.*

SALLY:	(*Softly*) Percy!
PERCY:	(*Swinging round*) Sally . . .

SALLY:	You—why you look just like Percy Piggott!
PERCY:	(*Incredulously*) In these old togs?
SALLY:	I like you in them. It's like old times—it makes me—almost happy.
PERCY:	I've always *wanted you* to be happy.

(*Reprise* " ORDINARY PEOPLE ")

PERCY:	Ordinary people like you and me,
	    Happy and contented as we can be,
	We can walk on air on our ordinary feet
	    Strolling hand in hand along an ordinary street.
	Ordinary people are we until
	    The ordinary time o' day is through

SALLY & PERCY:	When the ordinary moon is in the ordinary sky What extraordinary things we do!
PERCY:	(*Spoken*) You're not vexed with me?
SALLY:	Vexed? With you? What about?
PERCY:	Being broke and—well, what the newspapers say—and —everything!
SALLY:	Vexed? I'm *glad!*—Glad it's happened.
PERCY:	(*Amazed*) Glad?
SALLY:	(*Nodding*) Now you are broke, I can say something to *you* that I've been wanting *you* to say to *me* for a long time.
PERCY:	What's *that*?
SALLY:	(*After a pause, resolutely*) Percy—*will you—marry me?*
PERCY:	(*Flabbergasted*) Will I what?
SALLY:	Marry me. (*Breathelessly*) You've always been shy about coming to the point and I couldn't do anything—not when you were rich. People would have said I was after your money—but it's you I'm after.
PERCY:	(*Quite seriously*) But, Sally, this is so sudden.
SALLY:	*Will* you?
PERCY:	I don't know, Sally.
SALLY:	You don't know.
PERCY:	Just give me about five minutes to think it over . . . (*Looks at wrist-watch which isn't there*).
SALLY:	Five minutes? (*Furiously*) *Think it over! Think it over!* That a fine way to treat a girl (*Sobbing*) when she's made a fool of herself doing the asking.
PERCY:	You don't understand, Sally—what I mean is—give me just a few minutes—give me till *midnight!*

        ENTER CONNELLY *and* MOTTY *in his First Act suit L.2.E.*

SALLY:	I'll do nothing of the kind. If you don't know your mind now, Percy Gordon Kitchener Piggott, you never will.

Go on, marry anyone you like—*but don't you ever dare come asking me again!* Percival Gordon Kitchener Piggott!

EXITS into apartment. Slams door R.1.E.

PERCY: Sally! Sally, if I could only explain.

MOTTY: Hey, what's all this ? Have you two been quarrelling ?

CONNELLY: Good evening, Mr. Piggott. (*He crosses over to Stage R. behind* PERCY).

PERCY: Good evening, Mr. Connelly. My Sally's asked me to marry her—and, I had to say no!

MOTTY: She's asked you to marry her—why you good for nothing, blithering, extravagant, daft, gormless monkey!

CONNELLY: Mr. Whittle, please, it's just on midnight and I fancy that the young lady is going to have a pleasant surprise —that is (*Glancing at* PERCY) if everything is in order ?

PERCY: Aye, Mr. Connelly, everything's right with me.

CONNELLY: The whole million's gone ?

PERCY: Every nickel, every cent! (*Pointing to mantelshelf*) There are the receipts!

CONNELLY: You are now quite penniless? (*Connelly turns to mantelshelf and looks at receipts*).

PERCY: (*Proudly*) Absolutely! Flat stoney broke, in fact, I'm skint.

CONNELLY: Well, in that case—(*He fumbles in his brief case for cheque*) Mr. Piggott, it is my pleasant duty ... (*Takes cheque out and is about to present it.*)

ENTER BUDDY, *in evening dress, hurriedly L.2.E.*

BUDDY: (*To* PERCY) Percy, I thought you might be gone.

PERCY: Why, what's up ?

BUDDY: That twenty dollars you lent me on the yacht—here it is.

BUDDY *thrusts bills into* PERCY'S *hand. He gazes at it in dismay.*

CONNELLY: (*Sharply*) Twenty dollars! That's too bad.

CONNELLY *thrusts the cheque back into his brief case.*

MOTTY: (*To* PERCY *aggressively*) Hey, you borrowed that twenty dollars from me to lend him.

PERCY: (*Triumphantly*) By gum, so I did—take 'em.

PERCY *thrusts the bills into* MOTTY'S *hands and shows his empty hands to* CONNELLY.

PERCY: There you are, Mr. Connelly. Flat stoney broke.

CONNELLY: Capital! (*He takes the cheque out again*).

ENTER LILAC *L.2.E. hurriedly, she is in beautiful evening gown.*

LILAC:	(*Breathlessly, as she enters*) (*To* PERCY) Percy I only heard this morning and I've brought you this.
	LILAC *holds out packet.*
PERCY:	(*Frightened*) What's that?
LILAC:	(*Taking bills from packet*) Three thousand dollars. It's yours.
CONNELLY:	Three thousand dollars!
LILAC:	I sold that fur coat and *there's* the money.
	She thrusts the money into PERCY'S *hands.*
PERCY:	But it isn't *my* money.
LILAC:	(*To* CONNELLY) It *is*, Percy. Every penny of it.
CONNELLY:	Bad luck, Piggott.
PERCY:	(*Frantically*) But I don't want it—take it away.
	He gives money to MOTTY *and* BUDDY.
CONNELLY:	That won't do—you can't give it away.
PERCY:	Then I've failed. (*Twelve o'clock begins to strike on tubular bells in orchestra*).
CONNELLY:	(*Slowly and slyly*) Of course there is the matter of my legal fees!
PERCY:	It's too late—it's twelve o'clock, and I don't suppose that would be much—er—how much would that be?
CONNELLY:	Well, shall we say—three thousand dollars!
PERCY:	(*Quietly*) Three thousand dollars! Eh? Oh, Mr. Connelly, you're kidding—no you're not. (*He takes money back from* MOTTY *and* BUDDY *and gives it to* CONNELLY) Ee, your champion—here you are Mr. Connelly!
CONNELLY:	(*Handing* PERCY *cheque*) Congratulations Mr. Piggott on being the fortunate possessor of seven million dollars!!
	MUSIC CUE No. 25 FINALE.
ALL:	Seven million dollars!!
	The Tabs are opened at back revealing the ENSEMBLE.
	SWITCHBOARD CUE No. 48.
ENSEMBLE:	Happy New Year! (*They all run down and take up their finale positions*).
PERCY:	Sally, Sally. (*Shouting in direction of Door R.1.E.*) (SALLY *enters R.1.E. and walks R.C. to* PERCY). Oh, Sally (*taking her arm*) I couldn't tell you before, but under my Uncle's will I had to spend a million in order to make seven million dollars, and I've done it! Now I can say—will you marry me?

FINALE—THE PIGGOTT PENTHOUSE. Draw curtains along back mask sky-line background for all earlier sequences.

Act 2 : Sc. 10.

Chorus line-up from "Garter Girl."

Act 2 : Sc. 8(b). Sequence from "Garter Girl."

SALLY:	Yes, Percy!
PERCY:	And we'll go to Blackpool on our honeymoon!
MOTTY:	Aye—an' I'll come with you!
PERCY:	Nay, Motty—we can manage by ourselves this time!
FULL COMPANY SING:	" Should old acquaitance be forgot— For the sake of Auld Lang Syne."

CURTAIN.

After 4 Bars of Music

CURTAIN UP.   *See* DANCE PLOT.

ENSEMBLE waltzing and Principals waltzing down in pairs to take a call.

For 44 bars of " IT TAKES NO TIME " in waltz tempo, followed by 5 bars of " THE WEDDING MARCH " to bring PERCY and SALLY D.C.

CURTAIN DOWN

CURTAIN UP

CURTAIN DOWN

CURTAIN UP

PERCY hands down SALLY and MOTTY for a call, then he hands down LILAC and BUDDY for a call then SALLY and LILAC hand down PERCY for a call.

FULL COMPANY SINGING:

HALF CHORUS: " ZIP GOES A MILLION."

Zip goes a million—goin' to start a party
    Dish the dollars like a clown
Easy come, and easy go
    Don't be dumb—but spend all your dough
Zip goes a million—and a million million
    Percy Piggott's in town.

CURTAIN.

PLAY OUT MUSIC.

1 REFRAIN OF " ZIP GOES A MILLION."

SWITCHBOARD CUE No. 49.

DANCE PLOT

" Afternoon in Texas." Opening Number.
Curtain Rises after 10 Bars.
A Girl is sitting on a bench (S.R.). An old man is asleep on the steps
of the hotel. He wakes, as Cowboy shouts off stage and the opening
number starts with a boogie. The Chorus enter and a very bright number
is danced by Boys and Girls finishing with a Square Dance.

" Saving Up For Sally "
Percy sings verse and chorus. Small movement from Girls during
this. During second verse, no movement. On next chorus they walk
across stage and form semi-circle. Next chorus cross again and finish
number in two lines either side of Percy.

" Zip Goes A Million "
Everyone enters when Percy calls. Sally, Motty, carrying mugs.
Percy sings verse and Boys form semi-circle around him. On the chorus
everyone walks down to the footlights. Tabs close behind them. Percy
sings another verse. Everyone sings next chorus and do ensemble
movement. Blackout.

Rehearsal Scene. *Rehearsal Step.*
16 bars of modern ballet which is interrupted by Motty and then
Percy.

Rehearsal Scene. *Chiquita.*
Number starts with Lilac singing and playing castanets. She does
a tap dance and is joined by 5 Harlem People, 3 girls, 2 boys. She does
a boogie. They go off and a birdseller comes on, does 16 bars on point.
She exits. Lilac does a butterfly mime dance. Bobby Soxers enter
followed by the Doxis, then Boxers enter. There is a fight (4 girls
make boxing ring with a rope). One gets knocked out. Lilac is watching
this and the attention is switched back to her, when she shouts " Ollay "
louder than anyone. She vamps the Champ, who passes out at her feet.
There is a general bright movement from everyone. Lilac finishes by
doing 20 foutte turns with chorus in 2 oblique lines either side.

Office Ballet.
As Tabs open Head Stenographer gives cue for 4 girls who run down
stage and round desk. 6 Stenographers enter from O.P. Boys dance
down stage. They all busy themselves until P.D. Male runs on, tray in
hand, trips, somersaults and lands still holding the tray intact. He does
a solo, leaping on and off the desk S.L. and exits. Lift boy then does
a tap dance mimicing the typists. They type a rhythm and he taps it
out, then there is a general movement from everyone finishing with girls
on steps which have been pulled out of the side of desks. P.D. Male
rushes on, trips and lands with his head in waste paper basket.

Island Scene. *Ritual Dance and Stick Fight.*
Curtain goes up on a still picture, one girl kneeling either side of
stage with a circle of girls round with a circle of girls round them beating

rhythm and swaying with circles travelling to the right. They kneel while 3 girls do solos.

Boys are watching from the ramp. They run down and fight with sticks. P.D. is declared the winner and he selects his girl. Sally enters and sings " Raratonga," girls and boys sitting on stage in groups and exit at end of number R. & L.

" THE GARTER GIRL."

Starts in front of Tabs.

5 Girls enter either side doing polka step. (They all have long sticks). Tabs open at the end of first chorus to reveal Lilac in a group of boys. She sings verse and chorus.

The boys carry Lilac upstage then exit while she dances with girls. (16 bars Offenbach) 8 bars stop time tap, 8 bars tacit tap. Boys enter and carry her off. Girls form arch with sticks, she re-enters, turns down the arch. 4 Boys cross 4 of the Girls' sticks and they lift her up sitting on them. Tabs Close and Garter comes down. There is an encore with Lilac and one of the boys centre stage. 4 couples either side for finale picture.

FINALE WALTZ.

Couples dance waltz for 4 bars, then form two columns either side of stage and principals waltz down in pairs and take a call. " Auld Lang Syne " is played and Percy and Sally come down while crowd cheer.

WARDROBE PLOT

PRINCIPALS

LILAC:

Scene 1.—TEXAS.
Turquoise skirt; 1 white blouse; turquoise bow; red ankle-strap slippers; straw hat, turquoise ribbon.

Scene 3.—THEATRE.
Black jeans; black jersey; Fur coat.
White Spanish: hat, suit combination, bolero, skirt (lined red), white tap shoes.

Scene 8.—GARTER GIRL.
Black velvet leotard, trimmed diamante and net drape; black suede gloves; black fishnet stockings; black strap shoes; diamond bracelets; diamond necklace; diamond earrings; silver sequin garter; black headdress, paradise plume.

Scene 9.—TABS.
Mauve evening cloak; black velvet dress; black court shoes.

Finale—
Lime sequin dress; double black gloves; double black court shoes.

SALLY WHITTLE:

Scene 1.—TEXAS.
Grey skirt; white blouse; grey jigger coat, check; cream gloves; black flat shoes; red beret; pink organdie dress; white belt; white suede court shoes.

Scene 2.—BARBER'S SHOP.
Blue poult dress, trimmed broderie anglais; white elbow-length gloves; blue and white hat; double white suede court shoes; white handbag.

Scene 4.—ALLEY.
Pinky beige tussore dress; black patent belt; black satin bow; short white gloves; black patent court shoes; white anglais cap; black patent sling bag.

Scene 5.—OFFICE.
Lime and white plaid dress; white handkerchief; double white suede court shoes.

Scene 6.—ISLAND AND YACHT.
Turquoise organza dress; white ankle-strap shoes; white straw hat.

Finale—
Double Scene 1.

PAULA:

Scene 2.—BARBER'S SHOP.
Crush strawberry dress and handbag; black velvet bow; elbow-length black gloves; black court shoes; black horsehair hat.

Scene 3.—THEATRE.
Black velvet dress with drape of organza and horsehair; long black gloves; black sandals; diamante earrings, necklace, straps, bracelet; evening bag, black and diamante; cigarette case.

Scene 5.—OFFICE.
Black crepe dress; double Scene 2 gloves, shoes; black coolie hat; black handbag; red coat.

Scene 6.—ISLAND AND YACHT.
White pique dress with coral pink sash; white suede court shoes; white straw hat; coral bracelets.

Finale—
Grey satin dress; grey satin stole, lined lime; long white gloves, grey sandals; pearl and diamante headdress; pearl necklace; pearl earrings.

PERCY PIGGOTT:

Scene 1.—TEXAS.
Grey flannel trousers; sports coat; dirty burberry; 1 yellow shirt; brown shoes; red tie; grey pullover; check cap.
Fur chaps; belt, holster, 2 pistols.

Scene 3.—THEATRE.
Black tuxedo; black trousers; black evening shoes; linen.

Scene 4.—ALLEY.
Double Scene 3.

Scene 5.—OFFICE.
Pale grey suit; white shirt, collar attached; double brown shoes; tan tie; white handkerchief; horn-rimmed spectacles.

Scene 6.—ISLAND.
White linen trousers; white shirt; white socks; 1 mauve wreath; set of leys.

Scene 8.—YACHT.
Red suspenders; black boots; brown braces; combs; patterned shorts; peak sailor cap.

Finale—
Double Scene 1.

BUDDY:

Scene 1.—TEXAS.
Blue trousers; black sports shirt; sports coat to carry.

Scene 2.—BARBER'S SHOP.
Blue suit; white shirt with collar attached; brown shoes; blue striped bow; white handkerchief.

Scene 3.—THEATRE.
Double Scene 2.

Scene 4.—ALLEY.
Dress suit; black socks and shoes; linen.

Scene 5.—OFFICE.
Tan suit; double linen Scene 2; green tie; double shoes Scene 2.

Scene 6.—ISLAND, SEA SHORE AND YACHT.
White sailor trousers; red coloured T shirt; white shoes and socks.

Scene 9 *and Finale—*
Double Scene 4.

MOTTY WHITTLE:

Scene 1.—TEXAS and all 1st half.
Navy serge suit; striped shirt; wing collar; black socks; black boots; black bowler; black umbrella; black tie; watch and albert.

Scene 6.—ISLAND and all 2nd Half.
Striped trousers, white flannel; Panama hat; double-coat, shirt, collar, socks, boots; garland of flowers.

VAN NORDEN:

Scene 3.—THEATRE.
Black tuxedo; black trousers; white dress shirt, collar attached; black bow; black socks; black shoes; black Homberg.

Scene 5.—OFFICE.
Brown suit; white shirt, collar attached; brown and white shoes; brown and white striped tie; pearl pin; white handkerchief; white socks; grey Homberg; 1 pair chamois gloves.

Scene 8.—YACHT.
White flannel trousers; blue blazer; linen—double Scene 5.

Finale—
Double Scene 3.

SMALL PART MEN:

Scene 1.—TEXAS—JED HARPER.
Light fawn cotton jacket; cream trousers; coloured shirt, collar attached; brown socks; belt; padding; grey wig; steel-rimmed glasses; old canvas shoes.

Scene 4.—ALLEY—TOUCH.
Flash American cream coat; flash American tan trousers; white shirt, collar attached; big bow; grey hat; brown shoes, flash American; white socks.
Scene 5.—OFFICE—PILOT.
Padded trousers; leather jacket; double linen; black tie; helmet; brown shoes.
Scene 6.—ISLAND—RADIO OPERATOR.
White linen trousers; white shirt with pocket; black tie; gold clip; white shoes; double white socks.
Scene 8.—YACHT.
Double Scene 6.

Finale—
Tail coat; dress trousers; stiff dress shirt; wing collar; white waistcoat; white tie; black shoes and socks; white gloves.
Scene 1.—TEXAS—CONNELLY.
Grey striped suit; white shirt; stiff turn-down collar; black socks; black bow; grey waistcoat; black shoes; white straw hat; watch and chain.
Scene 6.—ISLAND—CAPTAIN.
Beard and moustache; Tropical American Naval uniform: white coat, white trousers, peak cap; white shoes, white socks.

PRINCIPAL MALE DANCER:
Scene 1.—TEXAS—SHERIFF
Black cowboy boots; orange shirt; fawn trousers; brown belt; star.
Scene 3.—THEATRE—DANCE DIRECTOR.
Brown jeans; lemon-yellow T shirt; white socks; black shoes.
Broadway Ballet—
Turquoise dressing gown; American flag boxing shorts; face mask with yellow hair; red socks; red boxing gloves; boxing shoes.
Scene 5.—OFFICE—OFFICE BOY.
Grey trousers; turquoise pullover; white shirt, collar attached; black shoes—double; white socks—double.
Scene 6.—ISLAND.
Naked except for mauve jock-strap with red flowers; Hawaiian wig, black.
Finale—KELLY.
Commissionaire's uniform:—grey and yellow coat, grey trousers, striped waistcoat, peak cap; white shirt, lime bow.

2ND MALE DANCER:
Scene 1.—TEXAS—HANK.
Blue jeans; old shirt; canvas shoes.
Scene 2.—BARBER'S SHOP.
White overall, trimmed pink; grey trousers; black shoes.
Scene 5.—OFFICE—LIFT BOY.
Grey jacket, trimmed turquoise; grey trousers, double; black shoes, double; socks, double; white gloves.

Scene 8.—GARTER GIRL.

Black evening cloak, lined lime green; tail coat; black dress trousers; black shoes; black opera hat; black socks; white stiff shirt; wing collar; bow tie; white waistcoat; white gloves; moustache, black handlebar.

Finale—

Double Scene 8.

12 CHORUS MEN:

Scene 1.—TEXAS.

FIDDLER

Blue jeans; turquoise shirt; belt; tan and yellow jacket; cowboy hat, fawn; cowboy boots; beard and wig.

5 FARM HANDS:

5 blue bib and brace overalls; 5 check shirts, assorted; 5 old straw hats; 5 pairs old canvas shoes.

6 COWBOYS:

6 large felt hats; 6 pairs trousers, assorted colours; 6 check shirts, assorted; 6 mufflers, assorted; 6 brown leather studded belts; 6 pairs cowboy boots, assorted colours.

Scene 2.—BARBER'S SHOP.

4 MEN:

4 white overalls, trimmed pink; double Office trousers; double black shoes and socks.

Scene 3.—THEATRE.

DESIGNER:

Double blue jeans; lemon-yellow shirt; brown moccasin shoes; white socks; length silver lame.

2 SCENE SHIFTERS:

Khaki cowgowns; doube black trousers; black socks, double.

PIANIST:

Tan trousers; beige shirt, collar attached; tan check tie; brown belt; brown shoes; white socks.

MUSICAL DIRECTOR:

Grey trousers; cream shirt, collar attached; red tie; tan shoes; white socks.

FIREMAN:

Navy uniform:—coat trousers; double black shoes; double socks; black tie.

DRESS DESIGNER:

Blue trousers; red check shirt; brown shoes; belt; white socks.

Scene 3.—THEATRE—Second Part.

BOXING (SECOND):

Blue shorts; red jersey; mask with yellow hair; boxing shoes; padding.

FOOTBALLER:

White breeches; red jersey; face mask; white helmet; red stockings; white socks.

1st HARLEM MAN:
Puce and white striped suit; negro mask; puce hat, felt; dark brown gloves (for negro hands); white shirt; turquoise bow; turquoise handkerchief; white shoes.

2nd HARLEM MAN:
Turquoise and white striped suit; negro mask; turquoise felt hat; dark brown gloves (for negro hands); white shirt; red American bow; red handkerchief; white shoes.

BRONX BOY:
Turquoise jeans; red jersey and white stripes; face mask with red hair; black soft ballet.

SPARRING PARTNER:
Blue shorts; white jersey; face mask with yellow hair; white socks; boxing shoes; white boxing gloves.

*Scene 4.—*ALLEY.

2 POLICEMEN:
American uniforms:—blue trousers, blue shirts, black ties, belts and holsters, hats, truncheon; double black shoes and socks; tie clip.

Add: for *Scene 5.*
Jackets; white shirts; Sam Browns.

LEFTY:
Flash American: fawn coat, fawn trousers, mauve shirt (collar attached), red tie, brown hat, brown shoes, white socks.

*Scene 5.—*OFFICE.

6 MEN:
Grey trousers; grey American jackets; white shirts with collars attached; turquoise ties; horn-rimmed spectacles; black shoes; white socks—double.

3 MEN:
Turquoise trousers; turquoise American jackets; white shirts with collars attached; grey ties; black shoes.

3 MEN:
Grey trousers; turquoise jackets; grey bow ties; white shirts, collars attached; black shoes.

CHAUFFEUR:
Blue slacks, blue jacket; blue peak cap; white shirt, collar attached, double; black tie; brown leather gauntlet gloves.

*Scene 6.—*ISLAND.

7 AMERICAN SAILORS:
7 white sailor trousers; 7 white singlets or shirts; 7 doughboy caps; 7 pairs white canvas shoes.

1 OFFICER:
American tropical uniform:—white officer jacket, white trousers, white peak cap; white canvas shoes.

3 NATIVE DANCERS:
3 black wigs; ragged trousers—1 lime, 1 blue, 1 mauve; 3 pairs fawn soft ballet.

Scene 8.—GARTER GIRL.

11 MEN:
Black tail coats; black dress trousers; white waistcoats; white dress shirts; wing collars; white bow ties; black shoes; black opera hats; black cloaks, lined lime; black handlebar moustaches; white gloves; black socks; posies.

Finale—
2 FURNITURE REMOVERS:
2 khaki boiler suits.
Remainder of Boys double Scene 8.

Scene 1.—TEXAS.

16 CHORUS GIRLS:
16 Village dresses, with white frilly petticoats and white frilly knickers (as under); tan slippers, plus:—
  (1) fawn blouse, green skirt, brown belt, straw hat, long plait.
  (2) fawn dress with brown spots, big straw hat, 2 brown bows.
  (3) White blouse, green skirt, tan sash, large straw hat, lime bow.
  (4) tan dress, green spot pinafore, pale green bow.
  (5) blue dress with white spots, lime pinafore, 2 plaits, 2 lime bows.
  (6) red and white check dress, long plaits, 2 blue bows, white ankle socks.
  (7) brown underdress, turquoise pinafore, 2 coils hair, brown bow.
  (8) Cerise blouse, lime muffler, dirty green skirt, 1 back coil.
  (9) lime pinafore dress, white blouse, straw hat.
  (10) turquoise and white check dress, 1 red bow.
  (11) blue check blouse, lime skirt, tan belt, 2 lime bows.
  (12) maroon blouse, pink skirt, white belt, 2 pink bows.
  (13) pink dress spotted white, 1 curl, white bow.
  (14) fawn spot dress, tan pinafore, brown bow.
  (15) blue check pinafore dress, blue blouse, lime bandeau, white ankle socks.
  (16) green dress, mauve pinafore, bow.

Scene 2.—BARBER'S SHOP.

5 MANICURISTS:
5 white pique overalls, trimmed pink; 5 pairs pink court shoes.

Scene 3.—THEATRE.

12 REHEARSAL GIRLS:
12 pairs brown jeans; 3 lime jerseys and caps; 3 tan jerseys and caps; 3 turquoise jerseys and caps; 3 pink jerseys and caps; 12 pairs fawn soft ballet.

Scene 3.—BROADWAY BALLET.

3 BOBBY SOXERS:
With face masks including blonde wigs; black soft ballet, plus:—
  (1) red and white loose jumper, turquoise rolled-up jeans.
  (2) cerise and white loose jumper, royal blue rolled-up jeans.
  (3) pink and white loose jumper, turquoise rolled-up jeans.

G

3 HARLEM NEGRESSES:
With brown mask and hair, brown tights, brown gloves, black ankle-strap shoes, plus:—
(1) orange harlem dress, orange hair bow.
(2) turquoise harlem dress, turquoise hair bow.
(3) cerise harlem dress, cerise hair bow.

1 CHINESE BIRD SELLER:
Turquoise dress with white sleeves; face mask with black hair; cerise satin star for hair; turquoise block ballet.

4 BOXERS' GIRL FRIENDS:
With face masks with dark red hair, white spray on star, white ankle-strap shoes, long white gloves. plus:
1 cerise and white striped dress
1 blue and white striped dress
1 turquoise and white striped dress.

1 SCHOOLGIRL:
Puce and white loose jumper; royal blue rolled-up jeans; face mask; blonde wig.

1 YOUNG GIRL:
Turquoise skirt, lined red; white sweater; face mask; black soft ballet; white socks.

Scene 5.—OFFICE.
3 OFFICE GIRLS:
Turquoise cloth jackets with white collars and cuffs; pleated turquoise skirts; black suede court shoes.

6 OFFICE GIRLS:
Grey sunray pleated skirts; white silk blouses; diamond brooches; diamond cuff-links; black suede court shoes.

2 OFFICE GIRLS:
Turquoise cloth skirts; white silk blouses; diamond brooches; diamond cuff-links; black court shoes; turquoise hats.

4 OFFICE GIRLS:
Turquoise cloth skirts; turquoise Eton jackets, trimmed silver; white collars and cuffs; diamond "P" brooches; turquoise hats; black court shoes.

Scene 6.—ISLAND.
16 HAWAIIAN GIRLS
16 pants; 16 dresses, assorted colours; 16 long black silk wigs with flower attached; double fawn soft ballet.

Scene 8B.—GARTER GIRL.
16 GIRLS:
16 mauve comb. suits, sequined black and silver; 16 mauve net sashes and drape attached; 16 mauve sequinned mittens; 16 mauve hats, sequinned black attached to lacquered wig; 16 pairs black fishnets; 16 pairs black satin court shoes.

Finale—
16 GIRLS:
16 evening dresses, all different styles, colours: lime, yellow and grey; jewellery to suit; lime or grey satin court shoes.

PROPERTY PLOT

Scene 1.   TEXAS.

    1 Armchair. 3 Cushions. (On Porch)
    2 Pots of Geraniums. (On Porch)
    1 Oil Lamp, Hanging. (On Porch)
    1 Flag Pole and Flag. (On Porch)
    7 Pairs Curtains. 7 Blinds on Windows.
    1 Armchair and 2 Cushions. (Down Stage O.P.)
    1 Low Bench. (Down Stage O.P.)
    1 Large Cactus Plant. (Below Door P.S.)
    1 Small Cactus Plant. (Up Stage P.S.)
    1 Ladder. (Above Door P.S.)
    1 Wooden Bucket. (Set on Stage)

Props Off P.S.—

    2 Suit Cases. (Buddy)
    1 Small Bag and Umbrella. (Sally)
    1 Bag and Mackintosh. (Percy)
    1 Black Bag. (Motty)
    1 Watch and Chain. (Motty)
    1 Phrase Book. (Motty)
    1 Brief Case. (Lawyer)
      Packet Dollar Bills. (Lawyer)
    1 Script. (Buddy)
    1 Prop Apple and Book.

Props Off O.P.—

    2 Magnums Champagne
  30 Drinking Mugs
    2 Revolvers and Holsters, Loaded (Percy)
    1 Fiddle and Bow

Off P.S.—

    Motor Horn effect

Scene 2.   BARBER'S SHOP.

Set on Stage—

    1 Wicker Lamp Post; 2 Iron Chairs with Ashtrays; 2 Iron High Stools; 1 Iron Low Stool; 2 Picture Books; 1 Pink Manicure Tray; 1 Silver Coin.

Off Stage P.S.—

    1 Shoe Shine Box with Brushes and Duster.

Scene 3.

Set on Stage—

    2 Large Wooden Boxes ⎫
    1 Small Wooden Box ⎬ Set back of Stage.
    3 Hampers   ⎭
    1 Long Bench
    1 Piano down stage P.S.
    1 Chair down stage P.S.
    1 Bentwood Chair down stage O.P.

Set on Piano—
Music; Ashtray; Newspaper; Matches; Cigarette; Bottle Coca Cola.

Props off O.P.—
Material for Dress Designer; Scent Spray; 2 Cigarettes and Matches (Buddy); 1 Scene Design.

SCENE 3A

Props Off P.S.—
1 Wicker Yoke with 6 Bird Cages; 2 Long Pieces Rope.

SCENE 4.   ALLEY.

Set on Stage—
1 Wooden Box.

Props Off Stage—
1 Wallet (Motty); 2 Revolvers, Holsters, Belts; 2 Police Whistles; 2 Police Truncheons.

SCENE 5.   OFFICE.

Set on Stage—
1 Large Writing Desk (Down P.S.)
1 Chair Behind Desk
1 Tape Machine and Basket (Side of Desk)
1 Large Settee, 2 Cushions (Down O.P.)
1 Small Desk behind Settee (O.P.)
2 Chairs behind Desk (O.P.)
1 Brass Bell on Desk (O.P.)
2 Rubber Plants (Up Stage by Lift)
1 Chair (Up Stage by Lift P.S.)
1 Trick Paper Basket (Side of Desk O.P.)
2 Iron Electric Fittings (On flat side of Lift)
1 Pair Curtains on Windows P.S.

Props Off O.P.—
2 White Telephones; 1 Large Glass Ashtray; 3 Gold Flit Sprays; 1 Gold Cigar Box and Cigar; 1 Gold Box Matches; 1 Gold Tray, Teapot, Milk Jug, Sugar Basin, Cup and Saucer; 8 Notebooks and Pencils; 4 Ledgers; 1 Pair Horn-rimmed Specs.; 1 Balance Sheet (Motty); 4 Boxes Roses.

Props Off Lift Doors—
6 Large Money Bags; 2 Prop Typewriters, 1 Bunch Flowers; 2 Machine Guns.

Props Off P.S.—
3 White Slings; 1 Blotter, Pen Tray, Pencil, Cheque Book (Sally); 1 Trick Tray, with glass and duster; 3 Green Writing Books; 4 Ledgers; 1 "New York Times."

SCENE 6.   ISLAND.

Set on Stage—
1 Rock Seat (Down P.S.); 4 Broomsticks; 1 Prop Dagger.

Off Stage O.P.—
1 Wicker Chair and Cushion; 2 pieces Rope; 4 Garlands.

Off Stage P.S.—
40 Garlands.

SCENE 7.   BOAT.

Wireless Room—
1 Table; 1 Wireless Panel Board; 1 Iron Swivel Chair; 1 Pair Headphones; 1 Morse Tapper; 1 Loudspeaker; Pencil and Paper; 1 Large Brass Lamp; 1 White Lifebelt on shelf over door; 5 Books on shelf; 1 Coat Hook on Flat.

Set in Cabin—
1 Rug on floor; 1 Large Cupboard; 1 Small Cupboard; 1 Wicker Chair; 1 Bed, Draw, Mattress, Pillow, Cover; 1 Trick Picture over bed; 1 Coat hook on Flat; 1 Single Curtain on rod; 1 Small Pair curtains; 1 White Lifebelt over door; Black Pencil (Operator); 2 Pieces Rope (Percy); 1 Bottle Whisky, 3 Glasses (On small Cupboard); Dirty Clothes on bed.

Props Off P.S.—
1 Red Lifebelt (Motty).

Off O.P.—
Thunder Sheet ⎫
  Crash Effect ⎬ Scene 9
Bomb Effect ⎭

SCENE 8.

Props Off Stage—
20 Black Sticks (for Girls); 1 Silver Stick (for Lilac); 12 Bouquets (for Boys).

SCENE 9.   BOAT.

Strike: Whisky and Glasses from Scene 7
Picture to fall on cue.

SCENE 10.

Set on Stage—
1 Pair Curtains, drawn; 1 Wooden Box marked " Sold. Lot 110 "; 1 Pile Papers on Box.

Props Off O.P. Down Stage Door—
1 Hand Grip and Mackintosh (Percy).

Props Off P.S.—
1 Large Envelope with Passport
3 Small Bundles Dollar Bills (Lilac)
1 Cheque (Lawyer)
Wrist Watch (Percy).

LIGHTING PLAN.

3 FLOODS ASIDE.

4 CIRCUITS

Batten 4	0	32	11	16	
Ground Row	1	32	11	16	
Batten 3	1	32	11	16	
Batten 2	1	32	10	16	
Batten 1	1	32	11	16	
Foots	1	32	11	16	
	W	B	A	R	

```
Colours
Required
 1   17      10   51
16   21      32   17
 3
```

1 Spot or Pageant aside on Stage if available.

Colours: 10 pink   For Stage
          7 pink   Pageants
         18 blue

SPOT BAR AND COLOURS. (Spots or A.A.s.)

51	13	51	18	10	51	51	10	18	16	51	18	51

F.O.H.
CIRCLE
SPOTS

1	1	32	32	10	10	51	51	51
1	1	32	32	10	10	51	51	51

Each set of colours to be evenly distributed across stage.

LIGHTING PLOTS.
SWITCHBOARD.
ACT I.

Circuits & Colours

Foots ...   1   11   16   32

          W   A   R   F

SCENE 1.

Batten 4 on backcloth. 32 Blue Full.
Battens 3, 2, 1 W.A. circuits ½ R.T.B. full.
Foots. All circuits full up.
Dips p.s. on backcloth. 2 Floods Top 17 Blue   ⎫
               Bottom 10 Pink ⎬ Full.
    p.s. O.S. entrance. 1 Flood. 16 Blue. Full. ⎭
Dips o.p. U.S. behind hotel on backcloth. 1 Flood. 17 Blue (full).
Dips o.p. D.S. in 1st entrance. 1 Flood. 7 Pink (full).
Dips o.p. Behind windows of hotel. 1 Flood. Open White (full).
All Dips full up.
    Spot Bar Full up.
F.O.H. All spots full up.
Cue   1.   Song: "Thing About You." Check everything 1/4 out
           except O.P. Dip. Open White Flood.
Cue   2.   End of Song. Fade everything back to full.
Cue   3.   1 Minute Fade. First fade in Lantern under veranda and
           Lantern on bracket. Follow on with Batts. and Floats.
           W.T.A. Circuits to out.
           Spot Bar to 1/4 out.
           F.O.H. to 1/4 out.
           Dips to 1/4 out except O.P.
           Open White Flood.
Cue   4.   Fade back.
           Spot Bar to full.
           F.O.H. to full.
           Floats W and A Circuits to full.
Cue   5.   D.B.O.

SCENE 2.

                   11
Cue   6.   Fade in Floats A Circuit to full.
                   32
                   B
          F.O.H.   11 pinks to full.
    Dips 1 flood.
    Full each side.
          Behind transparencies open white.
Cue   7.   D.B.O.

SCENE 3.

    Fade in Foots all circuits to full.
    Bats. 1 2 3 4 A circuits to full.
                B circuits to full.
    Spot Bar Nos. 1—12 full.

F.O.H.   All 11 pinks and 32 blues.   Full.
Dips p.s. u.s.   2 Floods
              in   7 pink (top)
Full up   2nd Entrance.   18 blue (bottom)
Dips o.p. u.s.   2 Floods.
    p.s. d.s.   2 Floods.   Top 16 blue; Bottom 7 pink.
Full up   Top 32 blue; Bottom 7 pink.
    o.p. d.s.   1 Flood.   11 pink.

Cue 8.   Fade out everything.   (This will just leave Limes).
Cue 9.   Fade in B foots.
          B batts. to full.
          Dips to $\frac{1}{2}$.
          Spot Bar Nos. 2, 4, 9, 11 to full.
          F.O.H.   32 Blues to full.
Cue 10.   Fade out.   Dips p.s. 7 pink flood u.s. 7 pink flood d.s.
          Fade out Dips o.p. u.s.   7 pink Flood.
          Fade in 16 Blue Foots.
Cue 11.   Fade out all dips.
          Fade out Spot Bar.
          Fade out 16 Blue Floats.
Cue 12.   Fade in Spot Bar Nos. 2, 4, 9, 11 to full.
Cue 13.   Fade all dips to $\frac{1}{2}$
          in
          Spot Bar Nos. 5, 7, 8, 10 to full.
Cue 14.   Fade in A Foots to 3/4.
Cue 15.   D.B.O.

Scene 4.

Cue 16.   Fade in A and B Foots to full (centres if any).
          Fade in F.O.H.   Blues to full.
Cue 17.   Fade in W Foots to 3/4 (centres).
          F.O.H.   Pinks to full.
Cue 18.   D.B.O.

Scene 5.

Cue 19.   Fade in Foots all circuits to full.
          Fade in Batts. 1, 2, 3.   W.A. Circuits to full.
          Spot Bar 1—12 full.
          F.O.H. 1—12 full.
          Dips p.s.   3 Floods on Window Backing.
          One above the other : Top 21 green; Centre 3; Bot. 51.
          Strip Light in Lift.
Cue 19.   Dips o.p. d.s.   1 Flood 51 Gold through Arch
          o.p. u.s.   2 Floods
                    Top on Backing 3
                    Bot. 21 Green through Bars.
Cue 20.   Everything to 3/4 out.   (Song)
Cue 21.   Fade back to full.

INTERVAL

ACT II.

SCENE 6.

Pre-set—

R. Foots ⎫
B. „ ⎬ at ½

B Batts. 1, 2, 3, 4 full
Spot Bar 2—45 98 11 Full.

Pre-set. F.O.H. Blues full.

Dips P.s. u.s. Ground Row. Pink and Blue Circuits on Backcloth. Full up. Ground Row 16 Blue Circuit in front on Sea Row.

P.S. U.S. 1 Flood. 32 Blue in front of cut Cloth. Full up.

P.S. D.S. 1 Flood 16 Blue on to pool.

(If available a spot or pageant with 7 pink cutting across stage onto chorus.)

Dips O.P. D.S. (if available spot or pageant 10 Pink focussed with frost on Red Flower Border).

Cue 22.   Fade in F.O.H. No. 1's.
Cue 23.   D.B.O.

SCENE 7.

Cue 24.   Fade in R. and B. Foots to full.
          F.O.H. Blues to full.
Cue 25.   Fade in W Foots to 3/4.
Cue 26.   D.B.O.

SCENE 8A.

          Fade in No. 2 Blue Batt.
Cue 27.   D.B.O.

SCENE 8B.

Cue 28.   Fade in A and B Foots to full.
          Fade in Batts. 1, 2, 3 A to full.
          Fade in Batts. 4 B to full.
          Spot Bar all to full.
          F.O.H. Pinks and Blues to full.
          Spot Bar 1—12 full.
                                        Top 32
          Dips p.s. u.s. 3 Floods: Central 16
                                        Bot. 21
                                        Top 32
Cue 28.   Dips o.p. u.s. 3 Floods: Centre 16
                                        Bot. 21
              Ground Row: 1 Section
                          1 Amber.
Cue 29.   D.B.O.

SCENE 8C.

Cue 30.   Fade in Bat. No. 2 Blue Full.
Cue 31.   D.B.O. (Detonator and Flash).

SCENE 9.

Cue 32.   Fade in A and B Floats.   Full.
          F.O.H. pinks.

Cue 33. D.B.O.
SCENE 10.
   Cue 34. " Snap in."
      Foots W.A. Full.
      Batts. 1—2 Full W.A.
      Batts. 3 and 4 Blue Full.
      Spot Bar 1—12 Full.
      Chandelier 3/4.
       F.O.H. 1—12 Full.
      Dips p.s. u.s. 2 Floods 32 Blue Full (Backcloth)
         p.s. d.s. 1 Flood 3 Amber in Entrance.
         o.p. u.s. 2 Floods 32 Blues Full (on Backcloth).
      1 Flood behind Backcloth.
      Centres Open Whites.

         CURTAIN.

CENTRE LIME PLOT
As used at Palace Theatre.

SCENE 1.

   Spot principal male dancer. 51 Gold.
   End of Ballet. Flood out.
   Spot CONNELLY p.s. as door falls.
   Flood for " Zip Goes A Million."
   Cue 1. D.B.O.

SCENE 2.

   Spot PAULA 51 Gold, O.P.
   Also SALLY for rest of Scene.
   Cue 2. D.B.O.

SCENE 3.

   Spot Principals 51 Gold.
   Cue. 3. Fade out, pick up LILAC 17 Blue Spot.
   Cue. 4. Change to Double 18 Blue.
   Cue 5. Change back to 17 Blue.

SCENE 4.

   Spot MOTTY. 51 Gold. On Entrance through door.
   Spot PERCY on entrance 51 Gold.
   Cue 6. D.B.O.

SCENE 5.

> 51 Gold Flood for Ballet.
> Spot Principals.
> Pick up Pilot P.S.
> Pick up Girl with Tea, O.P. to P.S.
> PERCY at Desk.

SCENE 6.

> Flood 32 Blue Opening.
> End of Ballet, Spot Principal Dancers.
> 7 pink.
> Pick up BUDDY, entrance centre stage.
> 7 Pink.
> Pick up PERCY on entrance in chair, 17 Blue.
> Cue 1. D.B.O.

SCENE 7.

> Pick up BUDDY p.s. 7 Pink.
> Cue 2. D.B.O.

SCENE 8A.

> Box Flood Ship open white.
> Focus on PERCY on entrance.
> Cue 3. D.B.O.

SCENE 8B.

> Spot LILAC as Tabs open. 51 Gold and follow.
> Cue 4. D.B.O.

SCENE 8C.

> Focus on PERCY throughout Scene.
> Cue 5. D.B.O.

SCENE 9.

> Spot LILAC, BUDDY Centre Stage for Song, 51 Gold.
> Cue 6. D.B.O.

SCENE 10 from

> Cue 7. Pin spot PERCY sitting on box.
> Spot PERCY and SALLY. Remain to end.

O.P. LIME.

SCENE 1.

> Flood 51 Gold. Spot PERCY on all entrances.
> Pick up Cactus P.S. when PERCY goes over.
> Cue 1. D.B.O.

SCENE 2.

Spot BUDDY 51 Gold (P.S.)
Cue 2. D.B.O.

SCENE 3.

Flood 51 Gold.
Cue 3. Fade out.
Cue 4. Spot Boxer 51 Gold B.O. as he falls.

SCENE 4.

Pick up Policemen. O.P. couch. No. 7 Pink. Off on exit.

SCENE 5.

Flood 51 Gold.
Spot Boys with Money Bags. Then flood.

SCENE 6.

Flood 32 Blue. End of Fight Spot Principal Man and Woman.
7 Pink. Then Spot SALLY 32 Blue.
Cue 5. D.B.O.

SCENE 7.

Spot BUDDY, 7 Pink.
Cue 6. D.B.O.

SCENE 8A.

Box Flood Ship. Open White.
Cue 7. D.B.O.

SCENE 8B.

Flood 11 Pink on Girls.
Cue 8. D.B.O.

SCENE 8C.

Box Flood Ship. Open White.

SCENE 9.

Spot BUDDY p.s. 51 Gold.
Cue 9. D.B.O.
Cue 10. D.B.O.

SCENE 10.

Flood 51 Gold when lights come up on Scene.

P.S. LIME PLOT.

SCENE 1.

Flood 51 Gold. Spot MOTTY. Spot PERCY and SALLY for song.
After SALLY'S exit remain on PERCY.
Cue 1. D.B.O.

SCENE 2.

Spot BUDDY 51 Gold for song.
Cue 2. D.B.O.

SCENE 3.

Spot Principals. Spot LILAC when she takes off coat, 17 Blue.
Cue 3. Change to Double 18 Blue.
Cue 4. Change back to 17 Blue.
Cue 5. D.B.O.

SCENE 4.

Spot BUDDY 7 Pink on entrance p.s.
Spot PERCY 7 Pink on entrance through door.
Cue 6. D.B.O.

SCENE 5.

Spot Principals 51 Gold.

SCENE 6.

Spot SALLY 7 Pink. Spot PERCY 17 Blue.
Cue 1. D.B.O.

SCENE 7.

Spot BUDDY 7 Pink.
Cue 2. D.B.O.

SCENE 8A.

Box in Ship. Open White.
Cue 3. D.B.O.

SCENE 8B.

Spot LILAC 51 Gold.
Cue 4. D.B.O.

SCENE 8C.

Box in Ship. Open White.
Cue 5. D.B.O.

SCENE 9.

Pick up LILAC o.p. 51 Gold.
Cue 6. D.B.O.

SCENE 10.

Cue 7. Pin spot PERCY centre stage. Flood for Curtain Calls
Principals.

FLIES HANGING PLOT

—— 28ft. 6in.	———— Skyscraper Back Cloth. Sc. 1ʊ.
—— 27ft. 6in.	———— Back Cloth. Sc. 3.
—— 26ft. 6in.	———— Back Cloth. Sc.1 (doubled Sc. 6).
—— 25ft. 0in.	———— Garter Girl Back Cloth. Sc.
—— 24ft. 3in.	———— No. 4 Electric Batten.
—— 23ft. 9in.	———— Floods.
—— 22ft. 6in.	———— Back Cloth. Sc. 3 "B"
—— 21ft. 9in.	———— Velvet Legs. No. 3.
—— 20ft. 9in.	———— Island Cut Cloth. Sc. 6.
—— 20ft. 0in.	———— Foliage Border No. 3. Sc. 1.
—— 19ft. 6in.	———— Velvet Border. No. 3.
—— 18ft. 9in.	———— No. 3 Electric Batten.
—— 17ft. 9in.	———— Back Flat with Tabs. Sc. 10.
—— 17ft. 0in.	———— Office Back Flat. Sc. 5.
—— 16ft. 6in.	———— Garter Girl Border. No. 2. Sc.
—— 16ft. 0in.	———— Acting Areas.
—— 15ft. 0in.	———— Foliage Border. No. 2. Sc. 1.
—— 14ft. 6in.	———— Island Border. No. 2. Sc. 6.
—— 13ft. 6in.	———— Velvet Legs. No. 2.
—— 13ft. 3in.	———— Velvet Border. No. 2.
—— 12ft. 8in.	———— No. 2 Electric Batten.
—— 12ft. 2in.	———— Ship Backing. Scs.
—— 11ft. 3in.	———— Chandelier. Sc. 10.
—— 10ft. 9in.	———— Acting Areas.
—— 9ft. 6in.	———— Foliage Border. No. 1. Sc. 1.
—— 9ft. 0in.	———— Island Border. No. 1. Sc. 6.
—— 8ft. 6in.	———— Hairdressing Saloon Cloth. Sc. 2.
—— 7ft. 9in.	———— Garter Girl Border. No. 1. Sc.
—— 7ft. 0in.	———— Velvet Legs. No. 1.
—— 6ft. 0in.	———— No. 1 Electric Batten.
—— 5ft. 3in.	———— Velvet Border. No. 1.
—— 3ft. 6in.	—— Acting Areas.
—— 2ft. 2in.	———— Ship Frame. Scs.
—— 1ft. 4in.	———— Stage Door Cloth. Sc.
—— 6in.	———— Sea Shore Cloth. Sc.
V	

——————————————————— Trailers.

———————————— Setting Line

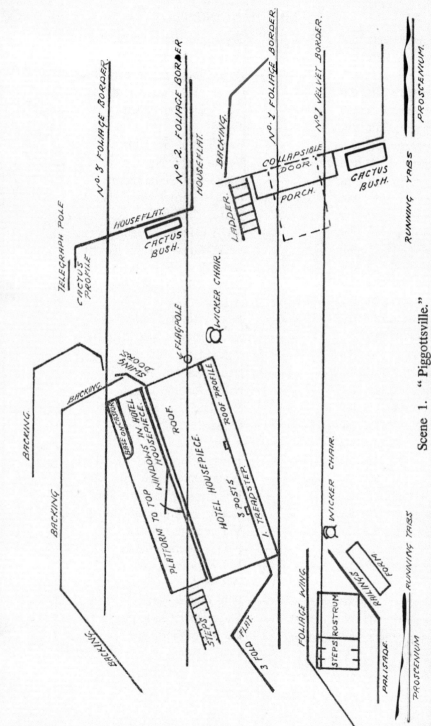

Scene 1. "Piggottsville."

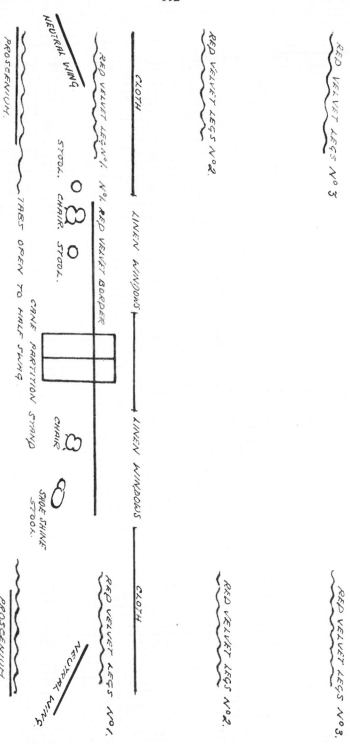

Scene 2. "Ritz Carlton Hotel, New York."

Scene 3. "The Stage of the Ziegfeld Theatre."

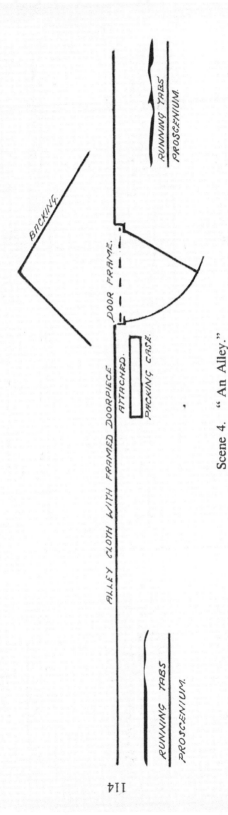

Scene 4. " An Alley."

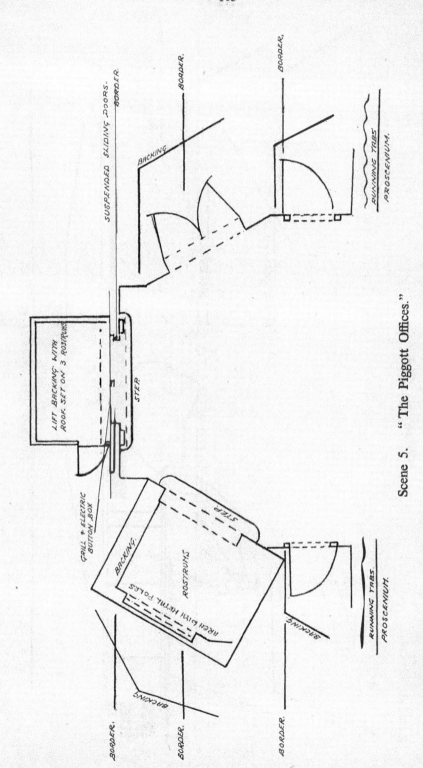

Scene 5. "The Piggott Offices."

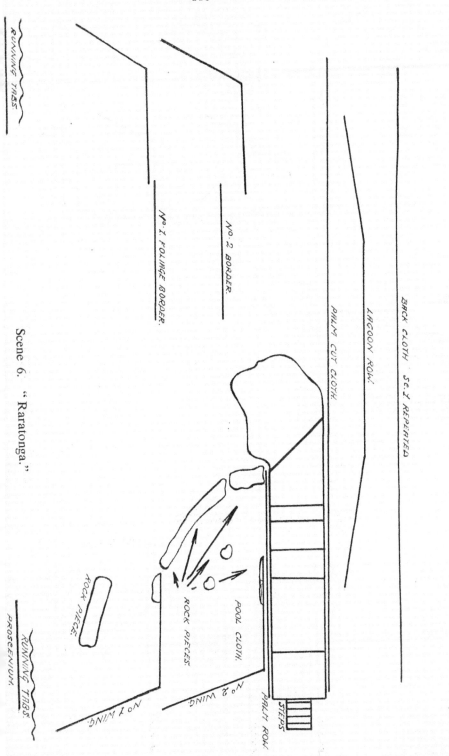

Scene 6. "Raratonga."

RUNNING TABS.

RUNNING TABS.

PROSCENIUM.

No. 1 FOLIAGE BORDER.

No. 2 BORDER.

PALM CUT CLOTH.

LAGOON ROW.

BACK CLOTH Sc. 1 REPEATED.

ROCK PIECE.

ROCK PIECES.

POOL CLOTH.

No. 1 WING.

No. 2 WING.

PALM ROW.

STEPS.

RUNNING TABS.

PROSCENIUM.

SEA SHORE CLOTH.

RUNNING TABS.

PROSCENIUM.

Scene 7. "The Sea Shore." Front Cloth.

Scene 8A & 8C. "Pleasure Cruise" (Rocking Boat).

Scene 8B. "The Garter Girl."

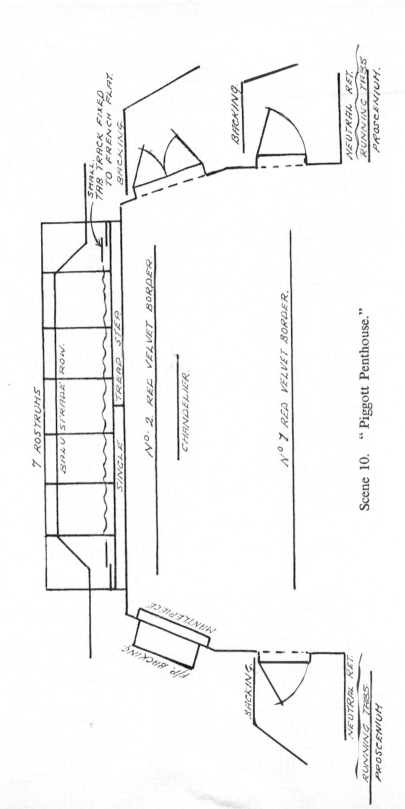

Scene 10. "Piggott Penthouse."